LORD THRING (1818-1907) was educated at Shrewsbury School and Magdalene College, Cambridge. After being called to the Bar he developed an interest in legislative drafting and in 1869 became the first head of the Office of the Parliamentary Counsel in London. He served as First Parliamentary Counsel from then until his retirement in 1886 and died in 1907.

MADELEINE MacKENZIE was born in Inverness and educated at Inverness High School and the Law School of the University of Aberdeen. Parliamentary Counsel since 1990, first in London and now in Edinburgh, she is a contributor to the 10th edition of *Craies on Legislation* (2012).

DAVID PURDIE was educated at Ayr Academy and Glasgow University. He is an Hon. Fellow of Edinburgh University's Institute for Advanced Studies in the Humanities, where his central interests are in the literary and philosophical components of the Scottish Enlightenment.

PRACTICAL LEGISLATION

THE COMPOSITION AND LANGUAGE OF ACTS OF PARLIAMENT AND BUSINESS DOCUMENTS

BY

LORD THRING KCB
LATE PARLIAMENTARY COUNSEL

THIRD EDITION

EDITORS

Madeleine MacKenzie LLB (Hons), Dip LP,
Parliamentary Counsel

Prof. David Purdie, MD, FRCP, Institute for Advanced Studies in the Humanities, University of Edinburgh

Luath Press Limited
EDINBURGH
www.luath.co.uk

First published 1877, John Murray, London
Second edition 1902, John Murray, London
Third edition 2015, Luath Press, Edinburgh
Reprinted 2016
Reprinted 2019

ISBN: 978-1-910745-11-3

The paper used in this book is recyclable. It is made from low chlorine pulps produced in a low energy, low emission manner from renewable forests.

Printed and bound by
Bell & Bain Ltd., Glasgow

Typeset in Mrs Eaves by
3btype.com

© Luath Press Ltd

CONTENTS

Foreword by Sir Geoffrey Bowman KCB QC 9
Editor's Preface to Third Edition 13
Introduction to Second Edition 15
Preface to the First Edition 31

CHAPTER ONE
INTRODUCTORY OBSERVATIONS

1 Mode in which a draftsman should prepare to draw Acts 38
2 Explanation of certain terms used in work 42

CHAPTER TWO
ARRANGEMENT OF SUBJECT-MATTER OF AN ACT

3 Difficulty of arrangement 45
4 Selection and statement of principles 45
5 Illustrations of selection and statement of principles in simple Acts 47
6 Illustrations of selection and statement of principles in complex Acts 49
7 Observations as to mode of framing principal and subordinate enactments 51
8 General rules of arrangement of Act, Rule 1 53
9 General rules of arrangement of Act, Rule 2 55
10 General rules of arrangement of Act, Rule 3 56
11 General rules of arrangement of Act, Rule 4 57
12 General rules of arrangement of Act, Rule 5 58
13 Summary of general rules of arrangement and observations 59

14	Observations on referential provisions where reference made to another part of the same Act....	62
15	Observations on referential provisions when reference made to other Acts	66
16	Observations on referential words	69
17	Observations on division of Acts into Parts and headings	70
18	Observations on marginal notes	72

CHAPTER 3
COMPOSITION OF SENTENCES

19	Clarity: object of parliamentary drafting	73
20	Enactment in its simplest form consists of legal subject and legal predicate	73
21	Mode of grouping legal subjects	75
22	Mode of grouping legal predicates	76
23	Mode of grouping independent enactments of a simple character	76
24	Mode of stating case	79
25	Mode of stating conditions	84
26	Mode of stating exceptions	86
27	Use of provisoes	89
28	Summary of Rules	90
29	Selection of words and other matters	90
30	Recommendation of use of generic terms	92
31	Enumeration of particulars	96

CHAPTER 4
GENERAL OBSERVATIONS

32	Preamble	99
33	Short title of Act	100
34	Extent of Act	100
35	Commencement of Act	101
36	Interpretation of terms	102
37	As to place in Act of definitions and certain other preliminary matters	103
38	Adjustment of existing and new law	103
39	Exemptions and savings	105
40	Schedules	106
41	Alterations during passage of Act	107

FOREWORD

The Parliamentary Counsel Office in London was established in 1869. Henry Thring (later Lord Thring) was its first head. He revolutionised the art of legislative drafting. For he brought order to statutes. In particular, many of them had been expressed in great slabs of unbroken prose. He established a system for dividing them into digestible portions and expressing them in a manner designed to promote intelligibility. And he set out his ideas in his book *Practical Legislation*.

In some ways the world of the drafter has changed radically since Thring's day. He tells us that he and Mr Gladstone would thrash out the intricacies of Bills together. It is difficult to imagine that sort of thing occurring in modern times. In other ways life remains much the same. He tells us about the criticism the drafter often suffers at the hands of others. This is a perennial occupational hazard. But he consoles us with the thought that 'virtue will, for the most part, be its own reward'.

As for the drafting itself, much of what he says has stood the test of time. He is concerned to secure that Acts are accurate, concise and clear. He says that 'clarity is the main object to be aimed at in drawing Acts of Parliament'. He says that the first task is to get the subject matter into your head, and he stresses that the whole art of clear and concise composition depends on the power of thinking. As he says, 'think before you write'.

He tells us that clarity is promoted by a proper structure for a Bill. Divide it into parts, divide the parts under separate titles, and arrange the clauses in a logical order. Separate the important from the detail. Make each distinct subject into a separate provision or series of provisions. Clarity is also promoted by a proper structure for individual propositions. So we should distinguish between the legal rule to be enacted, the case where it applies, any conditions subject to which it applies, and any exceptions.

He gives us other advice. Avoid legislation by reference so far as possible. Avoid Latin. Where possible without sacrificing accuracy, use ordinary rather than technical language. For law is made for man, not man for law. Repetition of the same word is not a fault if an ambiguity is avoided. The same thing should be said in the same words. Use generic terms to avoid repeating long expressions. Beware of the ambiguity arising from the lack of an adjectival inflection, as in 'a school or college subject to this Act'. And he advises us to learn the Interpretation Act by heart. That is a counsel of perfection which few will follow, though any drafter needs to be very familiar with the Act.

All this is not merely helpful. It forms much of the essential equipment of a drafter. And it is a tribute to Thring that the modern drafter takes it to heart as a matter of course, possibly unaware of where it came from.

The thinking on some other matters has changed since Thring's day. He espouses preambles and provisos, both of which are now out of fashion. He says that numbers should be written out at full length, as in 'section two'. That practice was abandoned long ago.

Other matters have undergone modification rather than rejection. The legislative 'shall' is now not so prevalent. Sometimes it is replaced by 'must'. Sometimes its imperative mood is replaced by the indicative, as in 'This Act applies to…'. Statutory language in general has become more colloquial and simpler. So a sentence might begin with 'But' or 'These are the factors to be taken into account'. Words like 'hereinafter' and expressions like 'the said officer' have died out. Clutter arising from excessive cross-referencing is avoided. And if cross-referencing is in fact used, words like 'above' and 'below' are often dispensed with.

Above all, the whole look of statutes has changed radically. Although Thring's precepts led to statutes being expressed in digestible portions, the statutes of his day can now look ponderous compared with modern ones. In particular, propositions nowadays tend to be broken up into shorter and neater sentences. It all makes life easier for the reader and it looks better.

These changes should come as no surprise. For legislative drafting is a constantly evolving discipline. Much of what anyone says about it should be regarded as recommendations rather than immutable rules. Just as Thring was bold enough to promulgate new techniques, drafters since his day have been bold enough to promulgate others. And long may that continue. For otherwise no improvements are made.

But let us not get carried away. Nobody could pretend that our statute book is perfect. As for Thring's book, some passages are heavy going. And (not surprisingly) some of it now looks decidedly old fashioned. And some of his wisdom lies hidden like nuggets in the earth and has to be extracted. Yet the book remains important, at any rate from a historical point of view. Why is that so? First it is the work of an actual practitioner in the difficult art of framing statutes who knew from experience exactly what he was talking about.

Second it demonstrates that, while all Bills are different and require different approaches, it is possible to recommend good practices. Third, when read in the light of modern practices, it illustrates how legislative drafting has changed over the years; and this in turn serves as a useful reminder that it is likely to go on changing. Finally the book has attracted an aura which transcends the sum of its parts and which emanates from Thring's authority and pioneering spirit.

The editors of this re-publication have wisely decided to keep Thring's vigorous and distinctive text intact. But they have added helpful footnotes to guide the modern reader. Anyone interested in legislative drafting will welcome the re-appearance of this influential work.

Sir Geoffrey Bowman KCB QC
First Parliamentary Counsel, London, 2002–06

EDITOR'S PREFACE TO THE THIRD EDITION

This third edition of Lord Thring's masterly work on legislative drafting is published to coincide with the Commonwealth Association of Legislative Counsel's 2015 Conference in Edinburgh. It also fulfils a long-held desire to see his work once again in print.

Thring's fame derives principally from the fact that he was effectively the founder of the Office of the Parliamentary Counsel in London, with his appointment as its head in 1869.[1]

I first encountered Thring's book in 1990, shortly after joining the Lord Advocate's Department in London[2] as a junior draftsman. Reading Sir Harold Kent's account of life as a draftsman in the Office of the Parliamentary Counsel[3] in Whitehall, I was struck by his vivid recollection of spending his very first afternoon in the office reading and absorbing Thring's book.

---

1 Thring (1818–1907) was First Parliamentary Counsel from 1869 until his retirement in 1886. For further information about Thring see the Editorial in the *Statute Law Review* (2007) 28.

2 The Lord Advocate's Department was a small Civil Service department, abolished on devolution in 1999. Its staff had the dual roles of drafting Scottish legislation for consideration at Westminster and supporting the Scottish Law Officers in their role as the UK Government's chief advisers on Scots law.

3 Kent, Sir Harold S., *In on the Act: Memoirs of a Lawmaker*. (London: Macmillan, 1979).

My interest was stirred, but investigation disclosed that the book had long been out of print. I was fortunate, however, to be able to borrow a copy of the book from the library of the Office of the Parliamentary Counsel, perhaps the very copy read by Kent on that first day.

I was struck by the practical nature of the advice given by Thring and by its timelessness. Although Victorian statutes are now often held up as examples of how *not* to go about drafting (largely on account of the length of the sections), Thring sought always to achieve the clarity and lack of ambiguity that are precisely the objectives of modern-day drafters.

In editing this edition, I have sought to make as few changes as possible, the aim being to supply the reader with Henry Thring's original text. Where strictly necessary, explanatory footnotes have been added.

My thanks to Professor David Purdie, my co-editor, for his help and encouragement.

Madeleine MacKenzie
Edinburgh
April 2015

INTRODUCTION TO THE SECOND EDITION (1902)

The following treatise was written many years ago for the instruction of the assistant draftsmen in the Office of the Parliamentary Counsel. It was published by her Majesty's Stationery Office, and being now out of print, is republished with the consent of the Government with an introduction and certain alterations required by recent legislation.

Mr Austin, no mean authority, writes in his work on Jurisprudence:[1]

> I will venture to affirm that what is commonly called the *technical* part of legislation is incomparably more difficult than what may be called the *ethical*. In other words, it is far easier to conceive justly what would be useful law, than so to construct that same law that it may accomplish the design of the law giver.

Mr Gladstone[2] expressed his opinion to me that a Bill was the very *soul* of legislation. One of the most learned men of

---

1 Austin, John, *The Province of Jurisprudence* (London: John Murray, 1832)
2 William Ewart Gladstone (1809–1898). British Liberal politician and statesman; born Liverpool to Scottish parents. Prime Minister four times: 1868–74; 1880–85; Feb.-Jul.1886; 1892–94. The UK's oldest PM, he resigned finally aged 84.

modern times, Bishop Westcott,[3] lately Bishop of Durham, has pointed out the essential requisites in drawing up Acts of Parliament – and indeed other sorts of serious composition. This he did when describing the benefits of his tuition by Dr James Prince Lee, the famous Chief Master of King Edward's School at Birmingham:

> If I were to select one endowment which I have found most precious to me in the whole work of life, I should select the absolute belief in the *force* of words, which I gained through the strictest verbal criticism.

For myself, I learnt from the instruction of those two great scholars, Dr Benjamin Hall Kennedy[4] and his brother George that even Greek particles can be made instinct with life and that words, though not 'built up in lofty rhyme and not expressing thoughts that burn' can be made to *breathe*.

After Cambridge, I passed to the study of conveyancing, that driest of all earthly studies, where I found that the apparent object of legal expression was to *conceal* the meaning from ordinary readers and that the forms which a law student of that period was incessantly employed in copying were wordy *cairns*. Upon these, each eminent conveyancer had from time to time thrown a new word, till the whole became a huge heap of unintelligibility.

Briefless, and therefore with much leisure, I devoted a great deal of time to the study of the contents of the statute

---

3   Brooke Foss Westcott (1825–1901). Bishop of Durham 1890–1901. Academic theologian and co-editor of *The New Testament in the original Greek* (1881); sometime Regius Professor of Theology, University of Cambridge.

4   Dr Benjamin Hall Kennedy (1867–89). Professor of Greek at Cambridge. Sometime Headmaster of Shrewsbury School (Est. 1552), where he taught the young Henry Thring.

book and here I found a great contrast between its earlier and its later pages.

That prince of all draftsmen, Stephen Langton, the Papal Legate,[5] expressed *Magna Carta* in short and precise language. For example, no-one can complain of ambiguity or verbosity in that most famous of all written enactments, which declares, when translated:

> To no man will we sell, to no man will we deny or delay, right or justice.[6]

The draftsman also, of the 22nd year of Henry VIII (c.9) (1531) left no room for doubt as to his meaning when he says, after reciting that the cook of the Bishop of Rochester had put poison into a dish of broth that he had prepared:

> Our said Sovereign Lord the King of his blessed disposition inwardly abhorring all such abominable offences... hath ordained and enacted by authority of this present Parliament that the said poisoning be adjudged and deemed high treason and that the said Richard for the said murder and poisoning of the said two persons... shall stand and be attainted of high treason and because that detestable offence now newly practised and committed requireth condign punishment for the same, it is ordained and enacted... that the said Richard Rose shall be therefore boiled to death, without having any advantage of his clergy.

---

5 Stephen Langton (c.1150–1228). Archbishop of Canterbury 1207–1228; a central figure in the dispute between King John and Pope Innocent III which contributed to the crisis leading to the signing of Magna Carta (1215). He divided the Biblical Chapters into the standard modern sequence.

6 The famous Article XL of Magna Carta (1215) which states:
Nulli vendemus, nulli negabimus, aut differemus rectum aut justiciam.

On the other hand when I came to modern times I found, again to quote Austin:

> statutes, made with great deliberation and by learned and judicious lawyers, have been expressed so obscurely or have been constructed so inaptly that decisions interpretating the sense of these provisions, or supplying and correcting the provisions *ex ratione legis*,[7] have been of necessity *heaped* upon them by the courts of justice. Such, for example, is the case with the Statute of Frauds which was made by three of the wisest lawyers in the reign of King Charles II, Sir Matthew Hale (if I remember right) being one of them.[8]

Ludicrous instances of confused expression occasionally enliven the pages of the statute book. Thus among the things which might have been expressed differently, an instance is to be found in the 52nd year of Geo. III (c.146). Penalties under this Act were to be given half to the informer and half to the poor of the parish; but the only penalty imposed by the statute was transportation[9] 14 years.

In a later instance, the art of the draftsman cannot be commended who gave as a definition in the Darlington Improvement Act of 1872:

> The term new building means any building pulled or burnt down to or within ten feet from the surface of the adjoining ground.

Amendments proposed to Bills have not infrequently erred in vagueness. Here is an amendment proposed by a QC in 1865:

---

7 Outwith the letter of the law.
8 Possibly. Hale's role in the 1677 Statute (29 Car 2 c 3) alongside Sir Francis North and Sir Leoline Jenkins, was challenged by Lord Chief Justice Mansfield in 1757.
9 To the penal colony of Botany Bay, Australia.

> Every dog found trespassing on inclosed [sic] land unaccompanied by the registered owner of such dog or other person who shall on being asked give his true name and address, may be then and there destroyed by such occupier or by his orders.

During the committee stage in the House of Lords of an Agricultural Holdings Bill, the following notice was put down by a noble Lord:

> To ask the Government whether they will consider the practicability of introducing into the Bill some provision for alleviating the great hardship now suffered by the family of any clergyman if he dies while occupying his glebe as many clergymen have latterly found themselves reluctantly compelled to do.

To qualify myself for avoiding, if possible, such pitfalls as these, I studied Coode's valuable book on legal expression,[10] and the American codes, especially those of Mr Field,[11] together with the code of procedure of the State of New York. I found that the subjects of Acts of Parliament, as well as the provisions by which the law is enforced, would admit of reduction to a certain degree of uniformity; that the proper mode of sifting the materials and of arranging the clauses can be explained; and that the form of expressing the enactments might also be made the subject of regulation.

I found also that these suggestions on the course to be taken to ensure clarity are not solely applicable to Acts of Parliament, but with a little adaptation may be applied to every sort of composition employed in business.

---

10 Coode, George, *On Legislative Expression* (London: Wm Benning & Co., 1845)

11 David Dudley Field (1805 – 1894). American lawyer and proponent of codification.

Having this in my mind but not having then reduced my conclusions to a complete system, I tried my 'prentice hand'[12] as an amateur in 1850 in framing a Colonial Bill for Sir William Molesworth[13] in which I endeavoured to simplify and shorten the expression of legal enactments. The Bill attracted some attention from the novelty of its mode of expression, but being opposed by the Government, did not become law.

In the year 1854 I had at last an opportunity of putting my new system in practice. Mr Cardwell, afterwards Lord Cardwell,[14] at that time President of the Board of Trade, was anxious to make a great reform in the merchant shipping law.

Following in some degree the example of the American codes, I divided the Bill into Parts and then divided the Parts under separate titles. I also arranged the clauses of the Bill in a logical order so that a glance at the table of contents would convey to the reader a correct idea of the effect of the Bill.

The clauses were drawn on a regular principle that divided the case, the legal action, the conditions, the provisoes and so forth. This was according to the plan which I afterwards fully developed and which is given in the following pages.

---

12 Thring quotes from Robert Burns's *Green grow the Rashes, O*:
    '... her prentice hand she tried on Man; and then she made the lasses, O!'

13 Radical politician. Colonial Secretary under Lord Aberdeen, Jul–Oct 1855.

14 Edward Cardwell, 1st Viscount Cardwell (1813–1886) Gladstone's Secretary of State for War. His 'Cardwell Reforms' (1870) abolished the purchase of Army Commissions.

Mr Farrer, afterwards Lord Farrer,[15] greatly assisted me in the preparation of the Bill. Being an officer of the Board of Trade, he was particularly conversant with the details of the subject and entirely drew the most technical part of the measure: that relating to seamen and wages.

I continued to be employed in drafting Acts of Parliament during my private practice at the Bar till 1861, when I was appointed Counsel to the Home Office, an office which was afterwards converted into the Office of the Parliamentary Counsel. For the remainder of my official life I was occupied almost entirely in preparing legislation.

It will be seen, therefore, that whatever deficiencies may exist in the following treatise they are, at all events, not due to ignorance or lack of experience.

It may be interesting to the reader to learn something of the mode in which a Government Bill is constructed. The best course will be to take the example of an important Bill such as the Irish Land Act of 1870.

The instructions given to me were, as usual, to a great extent verbal and were conveyed during a series of conferences with Mr Gladstone. I used to attend him at his house, generally by myself. I never hesitated to tell him my mind:

This will not do!

He would then stand up, his back to the fire, and make me a little speech urging his view of the case. I then replied shortly till the point was settled. I recollect on one occasion his manner was *so* vehement that I thought I must have gone

---

15 Thomas Henry Farrer, 1st Baron Farrer (1819–1899). Civil Servant and statistician.

beyond bounds in contradiction and began to apologise. He replied:

> Go on as you always have done and make no apologies. If my manner has led you to think that I am offended, I am sorry for it.

One limit, however, I imposed on myself. I observed that he objected strongly to what sportsmen call 'hunting heel'.[16] When a question had been fully argued and decided, he above all things disliked to have it reopened; and I never ventured to do so unless I could bring forward some fresh evidence on the subject.

Mr Gladstone was as economical of his time as he was of the public finances. I used to sit on one side of the table while he sat on the other side with a letter before him. When a difficult point occurred, I would say:

> Wait a moment and I will look at my papers.

While I was searching for the solution, Mr Gladstone would go on with his letter. When he saw me look up, he would again give his attention to the Bill. This would occur in a Bill involving the most intricate problems, such as the Irish Land Act of 1881, and he seemed to be able to turn his mind from one subject to another without the slightest difficulty or confusion.

Mr Gladstone's was the most constructive intellect with which I ever was brought in contact; and was also the most untiring in devotion to its object. He understood and revised every word of a Bill and even settled the marginal notes.

---

16 Hounds are 'hunting heel' when they hunt in the reverse direction of their quarry.

Once only did we have any discussion as to the *arrangement* of a Bill, and this arose on the Irish Disestablishment Bill.

I wished to put in one short clause at the very commencement — a sentence disestablishing the Irish Church. Mr Gladstone disapproved and I was about to accept his instructions to postpone the provision when Lord Granville[17] intervened, saying:

Had you not better pay attention to the *draftsman's* suggestions?

Mr Gladstone gave way and the proposed clause appeared at the beginning of the Bill.

A strange contrast to Mr Gladstone's management of Bills was that of Mr Disraeli.[18] He seemed to have an intuitive perception of what would pass the House of Commons, but he cared nothing for the details of a Bill. Once satisfied with its principles, he troubled comparatively little about its arrangement or construction.

It was in the course of preparing the 1867 Reform Bill and watching its passage every night through Parliament that I had ample means for the first and last time of judging Mr Disraeli's characteristics. I was constantly struck by his great skill in overcoming difficulties as they arose in Parliament and his tact in meeting the objections of his opponents by judicious compromises.

---

17 Granville George Leveson-Gower, 2nd Earl Granville (1815–1891). Liberal statesman; thrice Foreign Secretary and closest friend of Gladstone.

18 Benjamin Disraeli, 1st Earl of Beaconsfield (1804–1881) Conservative statesman, author and twice Prime Minister (1868 and 1874 80).

His courtesy to me never failed, even under the most trying of circumstances. My first introduction to him was so curious that it may be worth telling. I think it was on Wednesday, 13 November 1867 that Mr Walpole, then Home Secretary,[19] gave me to read a copy of the Reform Bill which had been prepared by a parliamentary agent. I expressed to him an unfavourable opinion on the Bill as drawn. This opinion was repeated to Lord Derby who sent for me to the House of Lords on Thursday 14 November. I told him in substance what I had told Mr Walpole.

Lord Derby said it was too late to take any steps to alter the Bill to the extent which I wished, and I undertook at his request to communicate with the draftsman and to tell him to proceed with his work. I returned to my office and was actually engaged in writing the letter when Mr Disraeli's secretary (now Lord Rowton) came in and told me as an instruction from Mr Disraeli to entirely redraft the Bill, adding that the Bill must be ready by Saturday 16 November.

Accordingly, next day I took the Bill in hand and, working with two shorthand-writers from ten till six, I completed it. The Bill was printed during the night and was laid before the Cabinet on Saturday. It was considered on Monday by Mr Disraeli who personally instructed me in the matter and the Bill was circulated to the House of Commons on Tuesday.

This *tour de force* in draftsmanship could not have been accomplished had I not been saturated, so to speak, with reform from my preparation of the Franchise Bill of 1866,

---

19 Spencer Horatio Walpole (1806–1898). Conservative politician. Three times Home Secretary in the administrations of Lord Derby.

when I prepared for the Government a complete series of memoranda and notes relating to the franchise. These included a comparison between the municipal and parliamentary franchises with a view to showing the advantage which would result from assimilating the parliamentary franchise to the municipal franchise. The work at the time had seemed to be useless, for the Franchise Bill of 1866 never became law.

The sum of the whole matter is this: to prepare a good Bill, the draftsman must receive sufficient instructions. These, however, will necessarily be short and he must exercise a very large discretion in filling up the gaps. He ought to draw up a memorandum and to supply notes furnishing the Minister with information on all technical points.

The Bill should be clear and should state at the very commencement the important principle of the measure. The greatest pains should be taken to separate the material from the comparatively immaterial provisions.

Before commencing to draw the Bill, the draftsman should ask the Minister on what questions he wishes to take divisions. These points should be placed at the beginning of the Bill in the clearest and most concise form so that it should not be possible for a division to occur on a complicated issue.

Above all, referential legislation must, as far as possible, be avoided. It is not fair to a legislative assembly that, as a general rule, they should have to look beyond the four corners of the Bill in order to comprehend its meaning.

It is, in my judgment, unwise to bring forward a Bill containing clauses which it is intended to abandon. The best way is to make the initial Bill as complete as possible, but to be ready to make compromises on certain points which the Government does not regard as essential.

As a detail, it may be well to warn the inexperienced draftsman against an intellectual danger incident to the employment of shorthand-writers. The essence of business composition is to think *before* you write, while the effect of employing shorthand-writers too soon is to induce the novice to write before thinking.

It may be well to warn the draftsman that, in his case, virtue will, for the most part, be its own reward. After all the pains that have been bestowed on the preparation of a Bill, every Lycurgus[20] and Solon[21] sitting on the back benches will denounce it as a crude and undigested measure, a monument of ignorance and stupidity.

Moreover, when the Bill has become law, it will have to run the gauntlet of the judicial bench, whose ermined dignitaries delight in pointing out the shortcomings of the legislature in approving such an imperfect performance.

Some judges, however, and these not the least eminent, have taken a different view of the position of the draftsman.

---

20 Lycurgus (fl. *c.*800–750 BCE) was the legendary lawgiver of Sparta who established its military-oriented society. His measures laid down the three Spartan virtues: equality among citizens; military fitness; and austerity.

21 Solon (*c.*638–*c.*558 BCE). Athenian statesman, lawmaker and poet. He is credited with having laid the foundations for the later Athenian democracy.

Mr Justice Stephen[22] said, speaking from his own experience:

> I think that my late friend, Mr Mill,[23] made a mistake upon the subject, probably because he was not accustomed to use language with that degree of precision which is essential to everyone who has ever had, as I have had on many occasions, to draft Acts of Parliament, which, although they may be easy to understand, people continually try to *misunderstand*, and in which, therefore, it is not enough to attain to a degree of precision which a person reading in good faith can understand; but it is necessary to attain, if possible, to a degree of precision which a person reading in bad faith cannot misunderstand. It is all the better if he cannot pretend to misunderstand it.

Now the real facts of the case probably are that the crude and undigested measure has for months occupied the time and thoughts of some of the ablest men in England assisted by their subordinate, the draftsman. Oftentimes, every possible objection to the Bill has been, as Mr Gladstone said in respect of the Land Law Ireland Act 1881, considered by the Minister before the Bill was brought into the House of Commons.

A Bill not involving any great constitutional change may meet the most determined opposition. Take the Army Bill as an illustration. The Army Act of 1881, like the siege of Troy, took ten years before it was brought to a conclusion.

---

22 Sir James Fitzjames Stephen, 1st Baronet (1829–1894). High Court judge and author. His book *Liberty, Equality, Fraternity* was a protest against John Stuart Mill's utilitarianism. He attacked Mill's essay *On Liberty*, arguing for legal compulsion and restraint in the interests of morality and religion.

23 John Stuart Mill (1806–1873). Philosopher, political economist and Civil Servant. He was an influential contributor to social theory, political theory and political economy.

Instructions were given to me by Mr Cardwell in 1867. A Bill was prepared, but was not proceeded with. In 1872 the subject was revived and a complete scheme was prepared for consolidating the Mutiny Act and the Articles of War. This scheme was partially considered by the War Office in 1873. It was then again laid aside till 1877, when a short interval of discussion occurred, after which it was again shelved until 1878, when a Select Committee, appointed by the Secretary of State for War, considered the Bill.

This committee gave a general approval to the Bill, and in 1879 an almost identical measure was at last introduced into Parliament — and passed.

Some idea of the labour involved in preparing this measure may be gathered from the fact that the papers written to explain the law *alone*, fill a folio volume of 1,067 printed pages. The Act was afterwards slightly amended and consolidated and under the title of the Army Act is annually brought into operation by a short special Act.

A short statement may be added as to the progress that has been made during the last 30 years in consolidation and codification and in the reform of the statute book.

With respect to codification, it may be stated at once that nothing has been done or perhaps *can* be done towards any systematic codification of English law.

With respect to consolidation and the reform of the statute law, however, more can be said.

In 1868 Lord Cairns appointed a statute law committee of which I am the only surviving original member. The duties of the committee are to make arrangements for, and to superintend the publication of, a revised edition of the statutes.

The first step was to free the statute book from obsolete and repealed statutes. This has been done under the superintendence of the committee down to the present time (1902). Two revised editions have been published. The second is a cheaper edition than the first and is contained in 16 volumes brought down to the year 1886, the last volume of which was published in 1894.

The committee also superintended the preparation of an index of the whole statute law, digested on a system laid down in instructions of great particularity from the committee to the compilers. This index is published periodically. The last edition was issued in 1901 and contains a complete analysis of the substance of the existing statutes.

With respect to *consolidation*, the committee has superintended the preparation of numerous Bills, some few of which have become law, but so great an opposition has been shown by certain members of the House of Commons to the passing of such measures, that further attempts to carry Bills of the kind has been abandoned for the present.

The recommendations given in these pages, though they are specially adapted to Acts of Parliament, apply with equal force to every description of business composition.

Whatever the subject, the writer should first get the whole matter into his head, separating the important points and trusting to his memory to retain them. He should then group his facts according to their importance, and when the outline of the composition is thus arranged, he may fill in the details by reference to the relevant papers.

It is very important for anyone engaged in business transactions to acquire the habit of trusting to memory till the whole subject is mastered. Making numerous notes weakens the thinking power, on the exercise of which depends the whole art of clear and concise composition.

Notes should be confined to references to passages which it is important particularly to *notice*. If a record is to be preserved for future use, then a Memorandum should be prepared.

PREFACE TO THE FIRST EDITION

OBJECT OF WORK

This work has been written as a practical guide for persons engaged in preparing Acts of Parliament. It is based on *Instructions to Draftsmen*, which have for some years been in use in the Office of the Parliamentary Counsel. Hence its didactic tone and its mention of various topics which would, if it were addressed to adepts and not to learners, be excluded as trivial and well known, but which are frequently neglected in practice.

SUMMARY OF CONTENTS OF WORK

It is divided into four parts.

The first part instructs the draftsman as to the mode of work, getting up his subject.

The second part deals with the arrangement of the subject-matter of an Act of Parliament, pointing out the expediency of presenting the law to Parliament in a clear and concise form, and insisting on the advantage of separating principle from detail, and material from comparatively immaterial provisions.

The third part is occupied with the subject of the composition of sentences.

The fourth part makes observations and suggestions with respect to preambles, the commencement and construction of Acts, and other formal matters.[1]

ABSENCE OF SPECIAL INSTRUCTIONS AS TO CODIFICATION AND CONSOLIDATION

As no special reference is made to Consolidation or Codification, it may be well to say in the preface a word on those subjects, and to point out the applicability to them of the rules laid down in this work.

MEANING OF CODIFICATION

Codification is the reduction into a systematic form of the whole of the law relating to a given subject, that is to say, of the Common Law, the Case Law and the Statute Law. Consolidation differs from codification in this alone: that it omits the Common Law and comprises only the Statute Law relating to a subject as illustrated or explained by judicial decisions.

SUMMARY OF PROCESSES ESSENTIAL TO CODIFICATION

Codification or systematic consolidation must be a gradual work.

1st. The Common Law must be extracted from the authoritative textbooks in which it is embedded, and so much as is not capable of being absorbed into the Statute Law must be digested into an Institute or Book of Maxims.

---

[1] The Interpretation Act 1889 has been printed at the end of this work, as it is the duty of every draftsman to know it by heart and to bear its definitions in mind in every Bill which he draws. The Act is not reproduced in the Third Edition.

2nd. The Case Law must be reduced into a manageable bulk by publishing leading cases (or cases which are in reality legislative decisions given by the judges) and by setting aside in a Digest the effect of such cases as are merely illustrative of Statute Law or Common Law, and are not readily incorporated therein, or by issuing an expurgated edition of the older Reports.

3rd. The Statute Law must first be indexed[2] and then be consolidated in classified groups. When the above-mentioned processes have been completed, a code will be readily made by absorbing into the text of the classified groups of Statute Law any portion of the Common Law or Case Law left outside the Institute of Maxims.

RESULT OF CODIFICATION A SERIES OF ACTS OF PARLIAMENT

It is unnecessary to enter into further details to show that the codification or consolidation of a particular branch of law is merely another mode of expressing the composition of an Act or series of Acts, embodying in the case of codification the whole of that law, and in the case of consolidation a portion only.

RULES APPLICABLE TO ORDINARY ACTS OF PARLIAMENT APPLICABLE TO CODE

The extent of the subject-matter, however, cannot affect the applicability of the ordinary rules of composition. Indeed, codification or consolidation is in many respects an easier task than the preparation of the amending Acts required for

---

2 This has been done. A chronological table, with an index to the Statutes, is published periodically by the Stationery Office.

current legislation. Just as it is easier for an architect to build a house from its foundations than to convert an old inconvenient house into a modern convenient one, so a draftsman can more readily construct an Act dealing with the whole of the subject-matter, than an Act in which the new law must be adjusted and made to harmonise with the old and often conflicting provisions of former Acts.

SLIGHT QUALIFICATION OF RULES AS TO ARRANGEMENT IN CASE OF CODE

The only qualification to be made in the application of the rules laid down in this work to a code or a consolidating Act, relates to the arrangement of groups of sections.

Thus, in making the plan for the arrangement of the sections of a code or consolidating Act, parliamentary considerations may usually be disregarded, and logical considerations, as they are called, be exclusively adhered to. This difference, however, is very slight, as in the great majority of cases the most scientific and logical arrangement is the one which is best for parliamentary purposes.

ARRANGEMENT OF CODE NOT TREATED OF

It must be admitted that no rules are found in this treatise for the arrangement among themselves of *groups* of statutes, whether such statutes are codes or merely consolidating Acts. In other words, no general outline of a code embracing the whole or a great part of the English law is laid down, or attempted to be laid down. This omission is designed, as any considerations *a priori* of the mutual relations of laws to each other, apart from convenience of administration, are too abstract to find a place in an elementary treatise, and may well wait for solution till the component parts of the code have been to a great extent completed.

ARRANGEMENT IMMATERIAL AS COMPARED WITH COMPOSITION OF ACTS COMPRISING CODE

Truth to say, promoters of codification would seem to be too much given to theoretical in preference to practical considerations. They spend much labour in determining the proper arrangement of a code before they have attempted to draw an Act or series of Acts embodying even partially any one branch of the law intended to be included in such code.

Yet, were the statute book once divided into a number of well-drawn Acts embodying both Statute and Common Law, all that would be required to make a code would be to group those Acts according to some convenient arrangement, probably according to the exigencies of the judicial or administrative departments of the Government. A good code is a collection of good Acts, in the same way as a good library is a collection of good books or a good gallery a collection of good pictures.

The exact arrangement of the several Acts in the code is of very little importance, compared to the excellence of the Acts themselves. In the same way, to continue the comparison, as in the case of a library or gallery the character of the books or pictures, far more than their relative arrangement, determines the value of the whole collection. Moreover, a good Index is in practice a not ineffectual cure for any defects in the arrangement of a code, a library or a gallery.

EXCELLENCE OF ENGLISH LAW IN SUBSTANCE THOUGH UNCOUTH IN FORM

Having thus deviated into questions of general legislation, it may be well to remark that the writer does not concur with the views of those critics who underrate English law, as compared with foreign codes, and who object altogether to parliamentary supervision of English legislation. Uncouth although it may be in form, English law is just and specific in its directions to an extent never yet attained by a foreign code. It leaves (and this is the practical perfection of law) less to the discretion of the judge than any other system of jurisprudence.

POSSIBILITY OF IMPROVING FORM WITHOUT INJURING SUBSTANCE

The real problem is to attain the advantages of a systematic code without destroying the fullness of expression and copiousness of illustration which characterise English law. That such an attainment is possible by gradual steps the writer has endeavoured elsewhere to show and he need not here repeat his views.

OBSERVATIONS ON PARLIAMENTARY SUPERVISION

With respect to parliamentary supervision, it is difficult to conceive a more searching scrutiny than an opposed Bill receives, in Committee, at the hands of Parliament. To dispense with such a scrutiny in the case of new legislation would be most unadvisable. On the other hand, the evils of parliamentary interference are no doubt seriously felt with respect to laws, the principles of which have been finally settled by the Legislature, and which it is desirable to codify or consolidate with a view to give symmetry to their form without alteration of their substance.

To such a codification or consolidation the House of Commons too often creates insuperable obstacles by reviving old subjects of controversy, and by insisting on discussing settled principles.

The duty of Parliament in such cases would seem to be to ascertain only that the new Bill correctly represents the old law. To effect this, all that is required would be to appoint in each House of Parliament a committee charged with the consideration of such Bills, and to have it understood that Bills, once approved by such committees, should pass without discussion.

It remains only to add that the writer was assisted in the work by Mr Jenkyns, the Assistant Parliamentary Counsel,[3] Mr CP Ilbert[4] and Mr GAR FitzGerald.

Other friends have also afforded great aid by suggestions and criticisms made during the progress of the work through the press.

Henry Thring
10 November 1877

---

3   Later Sir Henry Jenkyns KCB.
4   Later Sir Courtenay Ilbert KCSI.

CHAPTER 1

INTRODUCTORY OBSERVATIONS

In the following pages the term 'Act' will be used in place of 'Bill', and 'section' in place of 'clause', though an Act while in the draftsman's hands is more correctly termed a 'Bill', and its sections 'clauses'.

The reader must bear in mind that many of the Acts, notably the Merchant Shipping and Bankruptcy Acts, quoted as examples in the following pages, have been repealed or altered since this treatise was first written.

1 Mode in which a draftsman should prepare himself to draw Acts

When instructions for an Act are given to a draftsman, his first step should be to acquaint himself with the *whole* of the existing law relating to the subject-matter of the Act which he is directed to prepare.

COMPLETE KNOWLEDGE OF LAW ESSENTIAL

This completeness of knowledge is essential, for so complex are the relations of the various parts of English law that however limited the scope of an Act apparently may be, yet the law with which it deals may chance to be an offshoot of some larger branch of jurisprudence. Hence the draftsman, by the alteration of a definition or the introduction of a superfluous provision, may unintentionally subvert a settled principle of common law or disturb a series of legislative enactments.

Every Act in which a fine is imposed affords an example of what has been said. Various Acts define the mode in which fines are to be enforced, and award a scale of imprisonment to be inflicted in default of their being paid. A draftsman ignorant of these Acts will almost certainly contravene their provisions by altering the process for enforcing the fines or the scale of imprisonment. The draftsman must also as before mentioned be careful to bear in mind the Interpretation Act.[1]

METHOD OF GETTING UP LAW

If the draftsman approaches a subject for the first time, as a first step he will do well to endeavour to obtain a general view of its whole extent. This may be done by reading any modern treatise containing the law. The sooner, however, that he discards such a treatise, and has recourse to the original authorities, the more readily will his task be accomplished of arriving at an accurate knowledge of his subject.

In getting up the statute law, it is a convenient plan to obtain King's Printer's copies of the Acts[2] required and, tying them together, to read them through, beginning with the last Act and so on up to the earliest, striking out the repealed provisions.

---

1 See: the Interpretation Act 1978: An Act to consolidate the Interpretation Act 1889 and certain other enactments relating to the construction and operation of Acts of Parliament and other instruments, with amendments to give effect to recommendations of the Law Commission and the Scottish Law Commission.
2 The King's (or Queen's) Printer is a Civil Servant who is responsible for arranging for the publication of Acts.

In studying the case law, the best method is to discover the leading case on a given point, and having thoroughly mastered its principles, to pursue the law through all subsequent cases to the date of the last decision. A little practice, aided by an index of cases, will enable the student to complete his investigation very rapidly.

Cases readily range themselves into two classes, namely, those that lay down new principles, and those that merely illustrate the application of known rules. A reference to the headnotes will generally suffice to give a sufficient knowledge of an illustrative case, while a case laying down a new principle of law is, to the extent to which the principle is new, a leading case, and must be thoroughly mastered in detail.

This distinction between leading cases and illustrative cases is most important in reference to legislation. Leading cases constitute in effect judicial legislation, and admit of being codified by having their principles expressed in a legislative form. Illustrative cases are merely explanations or illustrations of the law. They may either be dismissed altogether by the draftsman or have their influence on legislation expressed by the insertion of a few words in a section to remove a doubt or explain a difficulty.

As examples of the difference between cases laying down new principles of law or judicial enactments and merely illustrative cases, take two decisions in relation to bills of exchange.

The negotiability of a bill of exchange was determined by a judicial decision. This decision, being followed, soon passed into the domain of settled law and, thus established, amounted to an enactment that bills of exchange are negotiable.

The decision in the case of *Rees v Warwick*, 2 B. & Ald. 113, on the question of whether a letter from the drawee to the drawer stating 'your bill £100 shall have attention' amounts to an acceptance involves no principle or general proposition of law, but is merely an illustration of the law in a particular case.

If the subject-matter of a proposed Act be very extensive, the general case law must be studied in a textbook, and the method recommended of going back to a leading case and tracing the law downwards must be reserved for such points as deserve to be set aside for special investigation due to their difficulty or importance.

In studying the common law, the earlier authorities, e.g., *Coke upon Littleton*[3] and Hawkins' *Pleas of the Crown*,[4] should be consulted in preference to more modern books. The common law having thus been traced to its origin, the later treatises may be looked at for the purpose of ascertaining, in a compendious manner, the numerous changes introduced by statute or by judicial decisions in almost every department of that law.

Whatever method of studying the law be adopted, the draftsman should as far as possible trust to his memory for collecting the results, making notes very seldom, and those extremely concise, in the nature of an index indicating where important propositions of law are to be found rather than in the form of extracts from or a statement of the law itself.

---

3 Coventry, Thomas, *A readable Edition of Coke upon Littleton*, (London: Saunders & Benning, 1830).

4 Hawkins, William, *A Treatise of the Pleas of the Crown*, ed. by J Curwood (London: Sweet, 1824).

By adopting this plan, he will acquire a habit of carrying in his mind a long and complicated set of provisions for a time sufficient to pass the whole in review. He will thus ascertain the true relation which the various parts bear to each other, a process essential to the completion of a clear and well-arranged scheme of legislation.

Where any considerable alteration of the law is to be effected, the draftsman will do well to keep a record of the law which he has acquired, and of the changes introduced by the Act which he is preparing. He should write a memorandum containing in concise terms the history of the law which he has been studying, pointing out the principal points in which his Act proposes to alter the existing law and adducing briefly the reasons for the alterations made.

2 Explanation of certain terms used in work

Before concluding this chapter, it will be convenient to explain the sense in which the expressions 'Act of Parliament' and 'enactment' are used in this work, and to point out the meaning of a division which has been made of Acts of Parliament into simple and complex Acts.

ACT OF PARLIAMENT

An Act of Parliament may for the purpose of this work be considered as a series of declarations of the Legislature enforcing certain rules of conduct or conferring certain rights upon or withholding them from certain persons or classes of persons.

This description of an Act of Parliament includes a principal Act with its various amending Acts, and this is intentional; for a series of Acts relating to the same subject is in fact, and ought for all purposes of arrangement to be treated as, a single Act of Parliament.

ENACTMENTS

The separate declarations of the Legislature contained in an Act of Parliament will be called Enactments.

It is possible, of course, that an Act may contain only one enactment, and in that case there is no distinction between 'Act of Parliament' and 'enactment'.

SIMPLE AND COMPLEX ACTS

Acts are referred to as simple and complex Acts. An Act is simple when its principle can be declared in one enactment and the whole of the Act is employed in working out that principle.

For example, the Stock Certificate Act 1863 is a simple Act, as the principle that a person may obtain a stock certificate is declared in a single enactment, while the remainder of the Act is occupied with showing how the principles declared in such enactment are to be worked out in detail.

On the other hand, the Land Drainage Act 1861 is a complex Act, as it deals in three Parts with the following different legal heads:

Part I. The issue of Commissions of Sewers for new areas on recommendation of Inclosure Commissioners;

Part II. The constitution of elective drainage districts on the application of certain proprietors;

Part III. The power of private owners to procure outfalls.

Again, the Irish Church Act 1869 is a complex Act as it consists (1) of the disestablishment, and (2) of the disendowment of the Church.

The above terms make no pretensions to logical accuracy, but will be found convenient for describing certain species of enactments and certain descriptions of Acts which practically must be dealt with by the draftsman as requiring different modes of treatment.

CHAPTER TWO

ARRANGEMENT OF SUBJECT-MATTER OF AN ACT

3 Difficulty of arrangement

Possessed of a full knowledge of his subject, the draftsman will, if the Act be a long one (e.g. the Irish Church Act 1869; the Landlord and Tenant (Ireland) Act 1870; the Land Transfer Act 1875; or the Explosive Substances Act 1875) feel himself bewildered by the multiplicity of the enactments and the extent of his task.

4 Selection and statement of principles

His first step must be, in the case of a simple Act, to settle the principle or leading motive, and in the case of a complex Act the several principles or leading motives of the Act on which he is engaged.

With respect to the mode in which the principle is to be selected, and where there is more than one principle in the Act the arrangement of the principles, the draftsman will, where an Act is of political consequence, be guided by the express instructions of the Minister. Before an Act of political importance is introduced, an able Minister settles in his own mind the questions on which divisions are to be taken, and forms a general idea of the mode in which those questions should be presented to Parliament. He then instructs the draftsman to follow his directions in these respects and to frame his Act in accordance with the leading questions to be submitted to Parliament.

In framing his instructions, the Minister will be greatly assisted by the draftsman laying before him a memorandum describing accurately the existing law. Such a document will clear the ideas of both the Minister and his subordinate.

In a simple Act, the principle when selected must be enunciated in its most concise form at the very outset of the Act either in one section or in two or more consecutive sections, as the subject may require.

In a complex Act, the principles should be arranged in different Parts of the Act, each Part of which should be treated as a simple Act, and contain its principle enunciated in the most concise form at the outset of the Part.

In short, the test of the arrangement of an Act or Part as respects the principle is this: If the reader, after mastering the first two or three sections, comprehends the whole drift of the Act or of the Part, the Act or Part is in that respect well arranged. The Act or Part is, as regards principle, ill-arranged in proportion as the principle is distributed throughout a number of sections, and broken up by conditions and provisions from which the reader has to extract it bit by bit.

This arrangement is to be recommended both for parliamentary and for practical reasons. It enables Parliament to decide at once on the principle of an Act unembarrassed by the consideration of details, and it places before the reader at the outset a clear view of the law intended to be enacted, without the confusing intermixture of the conditions under which – and the mode in which – that law is to be administered. The principle thus being settled, the conditions can be considered separately, and no confusion arises between objections of principle and objections of detail.

5 Illustrations of selection and statement of principles in simple Acts

The importance of selecting the principles and stating them in a concise form at the outset of an Act or division of an Act is so great that it will be illustrated by numerous examples, beginning with simple Acts and proceeding to complex Acts.

The simplest form of enactment is contained in one short clause.

For example, the Compulsory Church Rate Abolition Act 1868 provides in its first section as follows:

> From and after the passing of this Act, no suit shall be instituted or proceeding taken in any ecclesiastical or other court, or before any justice or magistrate, to enforce or compel the payment of any church rate made in any parish or place in England or Wales.

The passing of that clause abolishes compulsory church rates, and the remainder of the Act is taken up with providing for voluntary church rates, and making the proper reservations for cases in which money had been lent on the security of rates.

The Cruelty to Animals Act 1876, relating to vivisection, expresses its intention by declaring:

> That a person shall not perform on a living animal any experiment calculated to give pain, except subject to the restrictions imposed by the Act.

It imposes a penalty on any person performing any experiment calculated to give pain, in contravention of the Act.

Under that section, all experiments on living animals calculated to give pain are *prima facie* prohibited, and, as might be expected, the remainder of the Act is employed in declaring the conditions under which, in certain cases and for certain purposes, experiments may be performed on living animals.

Perhaps the best illustration of the concentration of the principle of a whole Act into one clause is found in the Succession Duty Act 1853, section 2, which is as follows:

> Every past or future disposition of property, by reason whereof any person has or shall become beneficially entitled to any property, or the income thereof, upon the death of any person dying after the time appointed for the commencement of this Act, either immediately or after any interval, either certainly or contingently, and either originally or by way of substitutive limitation, and every devolution by law of any beneficial interest in property, or the income thereof, upon the death of any person dying after the time appointed for the commencement of this Act, to any other person, in possession or expectancy, shall be deemed to have conferred or to confer on the person entitled by reason of any such disposition or devolution a 'succession'; and the term 'successor' shall denote the person so entitled; and the term 'predecessor' shall denote the settlor, disponer, testator, obligor, ancestor, or other person from whom the interest of the successor is or shall be derived.

This section embraces not only the whole subject-matter of succession duty, but that of the Legacy Duty Acts also, and the remainder of the Act is occupied in excepting successions subject to the Legacy Duty Acts and in illustrating particular examples of section 2, or in making rules for carrying section 2 into effect.

6 Illustrations of selection and statement of principles in complex Acts

A similar mode of arrangement is exemplified by complex Acts.

The Irish Church Act 1869 provides for (1) the disestablishment, (2) the disendowment of the Church. The disestablishment is enunciated in section 2, which is as follows:

> On and after the first day of January One thousand eight hundred and seventy-one the said union created by Act of Parliament between the Churches of England and Ireland shall be dissolved, and the said Church of Ireland, herein-after referred to as 'the said Church' shall cease to be established by law.

Nothing further was required to complete that enactment. The disendowment and formation of a new Church body occupy the whole of the remainder of the Act.

The Land Drainage Act 1861 consists of the following heads, divided in the Act into separate Parts:

> Part I. The issue of Commissions of Sewers for new areas on recommendation of Inclosure Commissioners.
>
> Part II. The constitution of elective drainage districts on the application of certain proprietors.
>
> Part III. The power of private owners to procure outfalls.

A reference to Part I (s. 4), to Part II (ss. 63 & 64), and Part III (s. 72) will illustrate the rule of enunciating in one section the principle of a Part of an Act.

The Ballot Act 1872 had two objects in view: the alteration of the law relating to the nomination of candidates at parliamentary elections; and the alteration of the law relating to the mode of voting. It was necessary to separate the essential conditions of the law from the detailed provisions intended to carry it into effect. Accordingly, section 1 lays down the rules for nomination, and section 2 creates a secret ballot with all its necessary conditions; while the detailed provisions required to give effect to a secret ballot are contained in a schedule of sixty-three articles.

In the Home Rule Bill of 1886, entitled 'Irish Government Act 1886', a good example will be found of the compression into a few sentences, at the beginning of the Bill, of the whole principle of the measure.

Section 1 declared that on and after the appointed day there should be established in Ireland a legislature consisting of her Majesty the Queen and an Irish legislative body.

Section 2 declared that, with the exceptions and subject to the restrictions in this Act mentioned, it shall be lawful for her Majesty the Queen by and with the advice of the Irish legislative body to make laws for the peace, order and good government of Ireland, and by any such law to repeal and alter any law in Ireland.

Then followed, in sections 3 and 4, the restrictions on the power of the legislative body, divided into two classes: first, the subjects on which they must not legislate; second, the principles which they were prohibited from adopting in legislation.

The prerogatives of the Queen with regard to summoning, proroguing and dissolving the Irish legislative body were defined in sections 5 and 6. It is obvious that if these six sections had been passed the Bill would have been in effect carried, as the remainder consisted of provisions necessary to give effect to so great a change in the constitution.

7 Observations as to mode of framing principal and subordinate enactments

Before concluding these illustrations it may be well to call attention to a difference in the mode of expressing the principle of an Act in cases where the principle cannot be enunciated in one enactment (as in the example of section 1 of the Compulsory Church Rates Abolition Act) but must range over several enactments. Where several enactments are required, there are two modes of dealing with the matter. Either the principle may be enunciated by itself in an independent enactment, without any words connecting it with its subsequent subordinate enactments, or the principle may at the outset be linked on by connecting words to the whole or to any part of its subordinate enactments. Similarly, the subordinate enactments may be expressed in words wholly unconnected with each other, or may be partially connected by words referring from one enactment to the other.

As an illustration of the first mode of dealing, take the Appellate Jurisdiction Act 1876. That Act declares, in four separate and unconnected sections:

1. the cases in which an appeal lies to the House of Lords;
2. the form of appeal to the House of Lords;
3. the attendance of a certain number of Lords of Appeal required at hearing and determination of appeals; and
4. the appointment of Lords of Appeal in Ordinary by her Majesty.

The second mode is shown in the principal and subordinate enactments found in the Land Drainage Act 1861, in which the section enunciating the principle provides, by reference to the subsequent clauses, that it must be made *on the recommendation of the commissioners*, and *on such application and subject to such conditions* as are therein-after mentioned.

Parliament, therefore, in passing the first section, pledged itself to require the recommendation of the Commissioners, and in a less degree pledged itself to the requirement of an application by the proprietors and to the other conditions of the Act.

On the other hand, in the case of the Appellate Jurisdiction Act, Parliament, in passing the first section, did not pledge itself to require a particular form of appeal or to require the attendance of the Lords of Appeal in Ordinary.

The selection of the one or the other of the above methods of dealing with a principal enactment accompanied by a series of subordinate enactments, depends on parliamentary considerations similar to those on which the arrangement of principles of law depends.

Sometimes it is expedient to fetter the principal enactment with a direct reference to subordinate enactments, in order to show that Parliament is not asked to carry the law beyond a certain limit. On the other hand, in many cases it is desirable to take the opinion of Parliament on the principal proposition in its barest form, and stripped of every possible detail that can distract attention, or lead to votes being given on a side issue, instead of on the principle involved. Such questions must be determined by the Minister, rather than by the draftsman, but it is impossible to overrate their importance, as an Act is not infrequently lost or won from a division being taken on the right point and at the right time, on a simple or on a complicated issue.

Where political and parliamentary considerations are not concerned, it is perhaps on the whole most convenient to introduce into the principal enactment references to the succeeding enactments, as the reader recollects a series of enactments when connected by referential words more readily than a chain of unconnected provisions.

8 General rules of arrangement of Act, Rule 1

Proceeding from the principle to the arrangement of the remainder of the Act, the draftsman will find himself assisted by the following rules, first, in sifting his materials in such a manner as to enable him to form a clear conception of the subject matter in hand and of the relations of its several parts to each other; and, secondly, in the practical task of arranging the sections of his Act and grouping them under appropriate headings.

Rule 1 — Provisions declaring the law should be separated from and take precedence of provisions relating to the administration of the law

Take as an example the Land Transfer Act 1875. It will be found that the provisions relating to registration of title are contained in the first four Parts of the Act, while the administration of the law stands by itself in the fifth Part.

The first part of the above rule is founded on the consideration that it is convenient for the purpose of clarity to separate the law from the authority to administer the law.

The reason for giving precedence to the law over administration is that until the law to be administered is determined, the proper authority to administer that law cannot be judged of.

Any verbal difficulty created by referring to the administrative authority before its constitution is stated may be avoided by the use on the occasion of the first mention of the authority of the phrases 'the Court by this Act constituted', 'the commissioners in this Act referred to' or other referential phrases.

The latter part of the rule, however, giving precedence to the law over the authority which administers the law is only applicable to a limited number of cases. Frequently the subject-matter is of such a character as to require the authority to precede the law.

Take, for example, the law as to coroners. The better mode would seem to be to create the coroner before laying down the law of inquest, on the ground that the law would seem to be an emanation from the authority, rather than the authority an institution established for administering an antecedent law.

A similar observation would apply to an Act relating to sheriffs. In short, the Rule is subject to so many exceptions that it is stated principally on the ground that *any* rule in so complicated a matter as legislation affords assistance to the draftsman, although it admits only of partial application.

A notable example of a case in which the above-mentioned Rule of putting the law before the administration has *not* been followed, is found in the Prison Act 1865.

That Act begins by declaring the local bodies on whom is imposed by common law or by statute the obligation to maintain prisons. It then proceeds to lay down the rules with respect to the appointment of officers, the discipline of prisoners and other matters relating to the prison, while it relegates to Part II the law of prisons.

The reason for this disregard of the general Rule was that in the particular case of prisons the law was altogether subordinate in importance to the provisions relating to the establishment of prisons. It was thought advisable to submit to Parliament the important questions relating to the maintenance and administration of prisons, in preference to beginning with the comparatively insignificant and little known provisions relating to the law.

9 General rules of arrangement of Act, Rule 2

Rule 2 — The simpler proposition should precede the more complex and in an ascending scale of propositions the less should come before the greater

For example, in an Act relating to offences against property, theft should precede theft with violence, or robbery, and so forth. Similarly, in dealing with the authority to administer the law, the less should precede the greater, the local the central, e.g., in the Public Health Act 1875 the local sanitary authority is dealt with before the Local Government Board.

This Rule also is in a great measure arbitrary and is suggested with a view to enabling the draftsman to form a clear conception of the relative bearing of sections, rather than to make it imperative on him to adopt it on all occasions.

Such a rule must constantly yield to political pressure, and the draftsman is frequently required by his instructions, or by the special circumstances of the case, to put the more complex proposition before the less complex, or the higher authority before the lower.

On the whole, however, experience suggests that the observance of the Rule leads to clarity and brevity in drawing. Uniformity in Acts of Parliament is of so much consequence that it is most desirable that some general rule of arrangement should be adopted wherever practicable.

10 General rules of arrangement of Act, Rule 3

Rule 3 — Principal provisions should be separated from subordinate provisions. The latter should be placed towards the end of the Act, while the former should occupy their proper position in the narrative of the occurrence to which they refer

Principal provisions are such as declare the material objects of the Act.

Subordinate provisions are such enactments as are required to give effect to the principal provisions by declaring in detail the manner in which they are to be worked out or by adding enactments to complete the operation of the principal provisions.

Taking as an illustration the Public Health Act 1875, the sections in Part II constituting sanitary districts and sanitary authorities are principal provisions; the sections in Part VIII altering the areas of districts and referring to the formation of united districts are supplemental provisions.

In the Representation of the People Act 1884, the law as to the extension of the franchise is set forth in the first five sections of the Act. Then follows, under the heading Supplementary Clauses, the definition of the franchise, the saving provisions, the construction of the Act and the Repeal of Acts.

This mode of arrangement will doubtless be objected to by persons who are desirous of acquiring a partial knowledge of an Act without reading the whole as being defective by reason of its not grouping under one head all the provisions relating to the same subject-matter.

It has, however, a twofold advantage: first, as respects Parliament, of submitting to the Legislature material provisions on which they may decide without being embarrassed with subordinate consequential regulations; secondly, as respects readers of the Act, by enabling them to obtain readily an intelligible view of the material provisions of the law before entering upon details involving no question of principle and interesting only to persons actually engaged in legal business.

11 General rules of arrangement of Act, Rule 4

Rule 4 — (a) Local or exceptional provisions, (b) temporary provisions and (c) provisions relating to repeal of Acts should be separated from the other enactments, and placed by themselves under separate headings

A good illustration of local or exceptional provisions is found in the Land Transfer Act 1875.

In that Act, the local registries for the counties of Middlesex and Yorkshire are dealt with at the end as separate subject-matters. By thus treating them as exceptions to the remainder of the Act confusion is avoided, and the provisions are found without difficulty, being arranged under a separate heading.

Examples of Repeal clauses are found at the end of almost every Act which disturbs existing statute law.

12 General rules of arrangement of Act, Rule 5

Rule 5 — Procedure and matters of detail should be set apart by themselves, and should not, except under very special circumstances, find any place in the body of the Act

The above-mentioned matters should either be enacted in a schedule, or what is far better (where possible) be left to be prescribed by a court or department of the Government.

For example, in the Companies Act 1862 the model regulations for a company are prescribed in the schedule; the rules for winding up companies are directed to be framed by the court.

By the Merchant Shipping Act Amendment Act 1862, section 25, the Queen can by Order in Council make regulations as to lights, fog signals and sailing rules, while in other Merchant Shipping Acts, the Board of Trade takes large powers of making orders for regulating the mercantile marine.

In the Trade Marks Registration Act 1875, the principles only of the registration are laid down in the Act, while the general rules pointing out the mode of registry and the classification of trade marks are directed to be made by the Lord Chancellor.

The adoption of the system of confining the attention of Parliament to material provisions only, and leaving details to be settled departmentally, is probably the only mode in which parliamentary government can, as respects its legislative functions, be satisfactorily carried on.

The province of Parliament is to decide material questions affecting the public interest, and the more procedure and subordinate matters can be withdrawn from their cognisance, the greater will be the time afforded for the consideration of the more serious questions involved in legislation.

Any attempt to evade the vigilance of Parliament by relegating to departments important matters can always be prevented by requiring the rules made to be laid before Parliament before they come into force.

13 Summary of general rules of arrangement and observations

Bearing in mind the above Rules, it may be useful to state as the result of the examination of a great number of Acts of Parliament that, though the subject-matter of the law is different, the subsidiary provisions for carrying that law into effect admit of being classified under a few heads.

The draftsman will find the following enumeration useful as a guide in sifting the complicated materials often presented to him for framing an Act and also in arranging the Act itself.

The arrangement, then, of an Act should be as follows:

1. The law or leading principle of the Act.
2. Administration of the law.
   a. Authority to administer.
   b. Procedure.
3. Penalties to enforce the law.
4. Expenses of enforcing Act.
5. Power to make by-laws.
6. Exceptional provisions.
7. Transitory or temporary provisions.
8. Saving clauses.
9. Definitions.
10. Extent of Act if limited.
11. Duration of Act if limited.
12. Repeal of Acts.
13. Short title of Act.
14. Application of Act to Scotland.
15. Application of Act to Ireland.

These rules necessarily not only admit of considerable variation but sometimes require it. They will, however, serve as a guide to the draftsman in ordinary cases.

One maxim he must steadily bear in mind, that whatever deviation may be allowed in the arrangement of principles and heads of law as between themselves, the essential conditions of a well-drawn Act of Parliament are that every principle of law and every head of law should be separated from every other principle and head of law. They should form the subject of a separate enactment or series of enactments, and in framing any enactment or series of enactments the principle or head of law contained in such enactment or enactments should be stated at the outset. The mode of giving effect to that principle or head of law should be dealt with by subordinate enactments, or otherwise according to circumstances.

Frequently, when the draftsman has sifted the materials of his Act according to the foregoing Rules, and is about to turn his attention to the enactments, he will find a difficulty in ascertaining their mutual relations to each other. In other words, the subject, although reduced in bulk, is still too large for him to classify throughout.

His course here is to work out separately and in complete detail each head of the law as if it constituted the whole subject-matter of the Act. Such a course necessarily involves a great deal of labour, but when the process is completed he will see the mutual relations of the several parts of the Act, and will frequently be able to generalise his Act to a degree he could not have anticipated until he had completed the separate groups.

Divide et impera[1] is the motto of a draftsman as well as of a conqueror. The one thing needful is to make each distinct subject the matter of a separate section or, if necessary, a separate series of sections. One should not, at the commencement, aim at conciseness when conciseness is placed in competition with, or in antagonism to, clarity of expression or fullness in working out the details of the law.

---

1 Divide and Rule. Originally, διαίρει καὶ βασίλευε. Attrib. Philip II of Macedon (382–336 BCE), father of Alexander the Great.

Having completed his arrangement of an Act, with the whole subject in his mind, the draftsman should scarcely ever alter it materially of his own accord. The consequence of such an alteration is to leave a confused outline of the law, which shows itself in the repetition or omission of necessary provisions, and in a hazy arrangement of the whole Act.

14 Observations on referential provisions where reference made to another part of the same Act

Before quitting the subject of arrangement, it may be well to notice a constantly recurring difficulty in planning Acts and constructing sections, namely, the determination of the best mode of dealing with legal subjects which require similar but not identical provisions.

No general rule can be laid down for all cases, but the following suggestions may be useful. Where the provisions of the principal subject are applicable to the subordinate, with few and well-defined exceptions, the best mode would seem to be to pursue the principal subject to its end without regard to the subordinate subject, and then to introduce a clause applying the provisions of the principal to the subordinate subject, with certain exceptions.

For example, the provisions of the Bishops Resignation Act 1869 were drawn as if they related only to English bishoprics, although it was intended from the first to extend them to the bishopric of Sodor and Man and to archbishoprics.

This application to the two subordinate subjects of the provisions relating to the principal subject is made by section 11 in the case of Sodor and Man as follows:

This Act shall apply to the bishopric of Sodor and Man in the same manner in all respects as if it were a bishopric in England, with the following exceptions:

1 If...

2 If...

3 The Bishop of Sodor and Man shall not...

And in the case of the archbishoprics by section 12 as follows:

A bishop coadjutor may be appointed in the case of an archbishop being incapacitated by reason of permanent mental infirmity from the due performance of his duties, in the same manner in all respects as if such archbishop were a bishop and his archbishopric a bishopric, and all the provisions of this Act shall apply accordingly, with the following additions and exceptions:

1 That...

2 That...

3 That...

On a similar principle, the sixth and seventh Parts of the Companies Act 1862 apply the Act to companies existing at the passing of the Act.

Where English Acts are intended to be applied to Scotland and Ireland, confusion is avoided by omitting all special Scotch or Irish terms in the body of the Act, and adding at the end: 'The provisions of this Act shall apply to Scotland (or Ireland, as the case may require) with the following modifications; that is to say...' and then setting out the modifications.

The use of a generic term with a defining clause will not infrequently prevent the necessity of overloading an Act with the enumeration of special provisions relating to particular local authorities.

For an example of this, the Contagious Diseases (Animals) Act 1869, section 9, may be referred to, which is as follows:

> For the purposes of this Act, the respective districts, authorities, rates, or funds, and officers described in the second schedule to this Act, shall be the district, the local authority, the local rate, and the clerk of the local authority.

Take the Act without this section, and endeavour to insert the various authorities into the text, and at once it will be found that almost every section requires a long list of names with special provisions interspersed.

Where a certain portion of the provisions of the principal subject are applicable to the subordinate subject without alteration, with some totally inapplicable, while others require alteration, the principal subject may be continued to its close, with the exception of the provisions applicable, with slight alterations, to both subjects.

The subordinate subject may then be introduced, and the former provisions, which are wholly applicable, to the principal subject, be incorporated by reference. Lastly come provisions applicable with slight alteration to the principal and subordinate subjects.

The fourth Part of the Companies Act 1862 illustrates the foregoing observations. The winding-up by the court is the principal subject. This is worked out to its close, with the exception of the provisions incorrectly called 'supplemental provisions', being in effect provisions applicable, with slight alterations, to the subordinate subject, as well as to the principal subject, which are postponed.

Then follows the main subordinate subject, 'voluntary winding-up', incorporating the powers of the liquidators (sections 133–137), which are specially drawn with a view to incorporation.

Winding-up subject to supervision comes next to voluntary winding-up and the differences, or rather the resemblances, between that process of winding-up and the preceding processes are stated in sections 148–152. Lastly come the 'supplemental provisions', making general regulations applicable to all three systems.

In whatever manner referential sections are arranged, great care and skill are required in making the referential words take up the principal enactments at the proper points, and the maxim that 'repetition is better than ambiguity' should be constantly borne in mind.

In any event, the draftsman should not be satisfied that he has properly accomplished his task until he has read through the principal enactments with the modifications proposed by the referential expressions and finds that, when so read, they effect the object proposed.

However great his difficulty, the draftsman must exclude any necessity for the adoption of the rule of '*reddendo singula singulis*'[2] or reading the sentences distributively. This is a rule which, like other rules of construction, has arisen from the obligation imposed on the courts of attaching an intelligible meaning to confused and unintelligible sentences. Referential provisions will naturally find a place at the close of the enactments to which they are referential.

---

2   Lat. 'Referring each to each.' Each term being applied distributively to its object. It is a variation of the doctrine of last antecedent.

15 Observations on referential provisions when reference made to other Acts

The referential legislation mentioned above, in which enactments in one Part of an Act refer to or incorporate wholly or partially enactments contained in another Part of the same Act, must be distinguished from referential legislation in which enactments in one Act refer to or incorporate wholly or partially another Act or Acts.

The last-mentioned mode of legislation is proper or improper according to circumstances. It is proper where the object of the reference is to incorporate certain general Acts, or parts of general Acts made for and adapted to incorporation.

For example, when powers of acquiring land are proposed to be taken, the Lands Clauses Consolidation Act 1845 must be incorporated with the proper modifications adapted to the cases of voluntary or compulsory powers of purchase.

Again, in all Acts imposing small penalties the Summary Jurisdiction Acts must be attracted.

It must be recollected that the Interpretation Act 1889, if not expressly excluded, so far as it is applicable necessarily affects every Act.

Other instances may be cited, and it is the duty of a draftsman to make himself thoroughly acquainted with all general Acts required to be incorporated, and with the best form of incorporating them. He ought not, without express instructions, to deviate from or modify the provisions of the incorporated Acts, which are well understood and are capable of being incorporated without creating any difficulty or raising any question of construction.

The advantages and disadvantages of incorporating a large number of Consolidation Acts will be best learnt by comparing a number of local Acts to which the series of Acts called the Consolidation Acts of 1845 and 1847 are applicable.

The advantages are that it secures uniformity of legislation and saves the time of Parliament. The disadvantages are that it reduces an Act to a mere outline, presenting to the reader no clear view of the law, and obliging him to fill in the details either from recollection or by a tedious examination of a number of distinct Acts.

No doubt the system as adopted in private legislation is inadmissible in public Acts in its full extent, but it must not on that account be wholly set aside. When the reference is to a distinct operation which is only subsidiary to the main objects of the Act, e.g. the purchase of lands in a sanitary Act, or the borrowing of money in a municipal Act, the possibility of referring to a distinct Act regulating such an operation conduces to clarity, and prevents the time of Parliament being wasted in considering unnecessary details.

It is the application of the principle of incorporation to cases to which it is unsuited, not its adoption in a great number of cases where it is useful, which is to be condemned.

The referential legislation to be always avoided consists in referring in one Act to provisions of another Act which do not readily lend themselves to incorporation, and require to be referentially modified before they can be made to harmonise with the incorporating Act.

An example of this description, to be noticed for the purpose of being avoided, may be found in the Nitro-glycerine Act 1869, section 6, which applies to searching for nitro-glycerine all the Gunpowder Acts relating to searching for gunpowder.

The subject of referential legislation ought not to be passed over without the addition of a few words condemning the practice of passing an Act which cannot be understood without referring to the enactments contained in some other Act.

This is done with a view to facilitating the passing of an Act through Parliament by partially withdrawing from the consideration of the legislature the subject-matter with which it has to deal. Such a system is calculated to make Acts of Parliament unintelligible to the ordinary reader who is, nevertheless, called upon to obey the law.

The observations of Lord Justice Mathew in the case of *Knill v Towse*[3] fully explain the inconveniences that have occurred from this kind of legislation as adopted in the Local Government Act 1888.

> The difficulty has arisen not from anything inherent in the subject itself, which is simple enough, and might be quite simply treated, but from the mode of legislation now usual in these matters. Sometimes whole Acts of Parliament, sometimes groups of clauses of Acts of Parliament, entirely or partially, sometimes portions of clauses are incorporated into later Acts, so that the interpreter has to keep under his eye, or if he can, bear in his mind, huge masses of bygone and not always consistent legislation in order to gather the meaning of recent legislation.

---

3   Law Reports, 24 QBD, 186, 195–6. The case concerned County Council elections.

There is very often the further provision that these earlier statutes are incorporated only so far as they are not inconsistent with the statute into which they are incorporated, so that you have first to ascertain the meaning of a statute by reference to other statutes, and then to ascertain whether the earlier Acts qualify only or absolutely contradict the later ones, a task sometimes of great difficulty, always of great labour — a difficulty and labour, generally speaking, wholly unnecessary.

It has, indeed, been suggested that to legislate in this fashion, keeping Parliament in truth in ignorance of what it is about, is the only way in which at the present-day legislation is possible. We know not whether the suggestion is correct; what we do know is that this procedure makes the interpretation of modern Acts of Parliament a very difficult and sometimes doubtful matter.

We, the judges, have perhaps the least cause to complain. We sit here for the purpose, among other things, of interpreting Acts of Parliament, and we bring, or ought to bring, to our tasks trained and experienced intellects. But in practical matters of everyday concern, such as the possession and exercise of the franchise, it is of the last importance that the law conferring it, and the rules which govern its exercise, should be easily comprehensible by the mass of ordinary voters.

We are well aware that protest as to past legislation is unavailing, but for the future to draw attention to a plain evil may perhaps be the first step towards its remedy.

The only remedy would seem to be that Parliament should persistently refuse to pass incorporating clauses unless they comply with the conditions above mentioned.

16 Observations on referential words

The expressions 'herein-before' and 'herein-after' and references to particular sections by their numbers, should be carefully avoided wherever practicable, for the position of sections is so frequently changed in the passage of an Act through the House of Commons that the expressions become inaccurate. Moreover the word 'herein-before' is frequently ambiguous, as sometimes it refers to the section alone in which it is found, and sometimes to the Act itself.

The above observation does not, of course, apply to referring in a subsequent Act to sections of an Act which has already become law, inasmuch as no alteration can take place in their arrangement.

17 Observations on division of Acts into Parts and headings

In conclusion, a few remarks may be made on the division of Acts into Parts, and the grouping of clauses under separate headings.

The first step in this direction was taken in the Consolidation Acts of 1845, which were most ably drawn by Mr Booth,[4] late Secretary of the Board of Trade, while holding the office of Counsel to the Speaker.

In these Acts separate groups of sections are prefaced with a statement:

> With respect to (*the subject-matter of the group of sections*), be it enacted as follows: (The sections forming the group being inserted without the introductory words 'And be it enacted that,' which, at that time, it was the practice to insert at the beginning of every section in the Act.)

---

4 James Booth CB (1796–1880). Barrister and Civil Servant.

The above plan of grouping sections may still be adopted with advantage where it is intended to enable provisions to be incorporated with other Acts (as was the case in the Consolidation Acts), or where in the same Acts certain provisions are to be applied to a different subject-matter.

The division into Parts, and the grouping under headings or titles, was adopted in the Merchant Shipping Act of 1854 on the model, in some degree, of the Code of New York. If used judiciously, it facilitates considerably the understanding of an Act. It is, however, a mistake to imagine that a mere mechanical subdivision into Parts insures clarity. In many recent Acts subdivision has been carried to excess.

As a general rule the division into Parts should only be used where the subject-matter of the Act involves different heads of law, each of which might without impropriety form the subject-matter of a separate Act, or contain classes of enactments such as 'Supplemental Provisions' or 'Temporary Provisions' distinct in their character from the rest of the Act.

It may be well to mention here that where it is intended to refer in the enactments themselves to the division into Parts, as for example by using the expressions 'this Part', 'Part five' or so forth, the Act itself should commence (as in the Merchant Shipping Act 1854 and the Companies Act 1862) by declaring that the Act is to be divided into Parts and specifying them. It will thus be out of the power of courts of law to refuse to recognise the division into Parts, as being a substantive portion of the Act.

The use of headings or titles dividing groups of sections also requires great care. If they are unnecessarily multiplied, they become little more than marginal notes. On the other hand, if clauses are grouped under them which do not properly fall within the description of the heading, the reader is misled instead of being assisted.

18 Observations on marginal notes

Marginal notes should receive more attention than is usually given to them. Each note should express, in concise form, the main object of the section on which it is made, or should at least indicate distinctly its subject-matter. All the notes, when read together in the 'Arrangement of sections', should have such a consecutive meaning as will give a tolerably accurate idea of the contents of the Act.

CHAPTER THREE

COMPOSITION OF SENTENCES[1]

19 Clarity: object of parliamentary drafting

Clarity is the main object to be aimed at in drawing Acts of Parliament. Clarity depends, first, on the proper selection of words; secondly, on the arrangement and the construction of sentences.

20 Enactment in its simplest form consists of legal subject and legal predicate

An enactment in its simplest form is a declaration of the legislature, directing or empowering the doing or abstention from doing of a particular act or thing. Such an enactment consists of a legal subject and legal predicate.

The legal subject denotes either the person directed or empowered to do or prohibited from doing the thing mentioned, or when the passive form is used the thing to be done or left undone.

The legal predicate expresses what the person is to do or leave undone or, when the passive form is used, what is enacted with respect to the thing to be done or to be left undone.

---

[1] See Coode's *Legislative Expression or The Language of the Written Law*, a work which draftsmen are recommended to read and to which I am much indebted in writing the instructions contained in this Chapter. [Coode, George, *op cit* (London: Benning & Co., 1845)].

If the law is imperative, the proper auxiliary verb of the predicate is 'shall' or 'shall not'. If it is permissive, 'may'.

For example:

Subject	Predicate
Every Court	*shall* take judicial notice of the seal of the Bankruptcy Court.
This Act	*may be* cited as 'the Companies Act 1862'.
A Sheriff	*shall not*, after the commencement of this Act, be liable for the escape of a prisoner.

The expressions 'It shall be lawful', 'It is the duty' and similar impersonal forms should not be used when the auxiliary verbs 'shall', 'shall not' or 'may' will do equally well.

Sometimes it is useful to substitute 'It shall be lawful' for the auxiliary form of expression, in order that verbs in the infinitive mood may be used in the dependent sentences.

The inclination of the Courts to construe 'may' as sometimes imperative in an Act of Parliament requires that in doubtful cases the draftsman should add words such as 'The Court may *in its discretion*' or 'may *if it thinks it expedient*' and so forth.

Where it is intended that a person should be exempted from the obligation to do a thing to which he would generally be subject (a very rare form of expression), it would be well to say 'It shall be lawful for A.B. not to do so and so' since the phrase 'may not' would imply a command that he should not do it. It is almost needless to add that expressions such as 'may and are hereby required' are redundant and should never be used.

21 Mode of grouping legal subjects

A number of legal subjects, legal predicates or independent enactments may be conveniently grouped together.

Useful formulae for uniting such groups of legal subjects are as follows:

Land Transfer Act 1875, section 5:

After the commencement of this Act the following persons (that is to say)—

[Legal subject No.1]

(1) Any person who has contracted to buy for his own benefit an estate in fee simple in land, whether subject or not to incumbrances; and

[Legal subject No.2]

(2) Any person entitled for his own benefit at law or in equity to an estate in fee simple in land, whether subject or not to incumbrances; and

[Legal subject No.3]

(3) Any person capable of disposing for his own benefit by way of sale of an estate in fee simple in land, whether subject or not to incumbrances,

[Legal predicate]

may apply to the registrar under this Act to be registered.

Merchant Shipping Act 1854, sections 322 and 323

The following offenders, that is to say—

[Legal subject]

(1) Any person who...

[Legal subject]

(2) Any person who...

[Legal predicate]

shall for each offence be liable to a fine not exceeding...

22 Mode of grouping legal predicates

Land Transfer Act 1875, section 118

[Legal subject]

The Lord Chancellor, with the concurrence of the Commissioners of her Majesty's Treasury, shall have power by general orders from time to time to do all or any of the following things—

[Legal predicate No.1]

(1) To create district registries...

[Legal predicate No.2]

(2) To direct, by notice...

[Legal predicate No.3]

(3) To commence registration...

[Legal predicate No.4]

(4) To appoint district registrars...

[Legal subject]

The Lord Chancellor may, with the like concurrence, from time to time

[Legal predicate]

make, rescind, alter, or add to any order made in pursuance of this section.

23 Mode of grouping independent enactments of a simple character

Independent enactments of a simple character may be linked together by any of the following formulae:

Companies Act 1862, section 133

The following consequences shall ensue upon the voluntary winding-up of a company.

Companies Act 1862, section 174

The registration of companies under this Act shall be conducted as follows; that is to say...

Land Transfer Act 1875, section 83

The following enactments shall be made with respect to registration of title.

Merchant Shipping Act 1854, section 103

The offences herein-after mentioned shall be punishable as follows; that is to say...

Sometimes a number of short enactments cannot conveniently be arranged in subsections, and in such instances they may be grouped in one section in the following manner:

Artisans and Labourers Dwellings Improvement Act 1875, section 5

[Enactment No.1]

The improvement scheme of a local authority shall be accompanied by maps, particulars, and estimates;

[Enactments Nos. 2&3]

it may exclude any part of the area in respect of which an official representation is made, or include any neighbouring lands, if the local authority are of opinion that such exclusion is expedient or inclusion is necessary for making their scheme efficient for sanitary purposes;

[Enactment No 4]

it may also provide for widening any existing approaches to the unhealthy area or otherwise for opening out the same for the purposes of ventilation or health;

[Enactment No 5]

also it shall distinguish the lands proposed to be taken compulsorily, and shall provide for the accommodation of at the least as many persons of the working class as may be displaced in the area with respect to which the scheme is proposed, in suitable dwellings, which, unless there are any special reasons to the contrary, shall be situate within the limits of the same area, or in the vicinity thereof;

[Enactment No 6]

it shall also provide for proper sanitary arrangements;

[Enactment No 7]

it may also provide for such scheme or any part thereof being carried out and effected by the person entitled to the first estate of freehold in any property subject to the scheme or with the concurrence of such person, under the superintendence and control of the local authority, and upon such terms and conditions to be embodied in the scheme as may be agreed upon between the local authority and such person.

An instance of the advantage of grouping enactments in a matter of some complexity may be found in section 10 of the Irish Church Act 1869:

When the annual sums herein-after mentioned cease to be paid, compensation shall be made in respect thereof by payment of capital sums as follows; that is to say,

(1) In respect of the annual sum paid out, &c, by payment of the capital sum herein-after mentioned, to...

(2) In respect of the several annual sums paid out of, &c. (such sums to be ascertained on an average of such number of years as the Commissioners may think fit), by payment of the capital sums herein-after mentioned, to...

(3) In respect of the several sums paid annually by, &c, by payment of the capital sum herein after mentioned, to...

(4) In respect of the annual sum paid out of, &c, by payment of the capital sum herein-after mentioned, to…

(5) In respect of the annual sums granted, &c, by payment of the capital sum herein-after mentioned, to…

(6) In respect of the buildings of the said college; by payment of a sum:

(7) In respect of the annual sums granted, &c, by payment of the capital sum herein-after mentioned, to…

(8) In respect of the annual sum paid, &c, by payment of the capital sum herein-after mentioned, to…

24 Mode of stating case

Little difficulty would arise in framing Acts of Parliament if the law were, as a general rule, meant to apply universally. It is, however, usually limited to special cases, and the first duty of a draftsman is to state clearly the nature of the case to which the law applies.

Where the case is simple it should be introduced at the beginning of the section with the words 'where' or 'when', 'in the event of' or 'if' with the indicative.

Companies Act 1862, sections III and 154

[Case]

Where any company is being wound up,

[Statutory declaration]

all books, accounts, and documents of the company and of the liquidators shall, as between the contributories of the company, be *prima facie* evidence of the truth of all matters purporting to be therein recorded.

[Case]

When the affairs of the company have been completely wound up,

[Statutory declaration (1)]

the court shall make an order that the company shall be dissolved from the date of such order,

[Statutory declaration (2)]

and the company shall be dissolved accordingly.

Where a single statutory declaration applies to numerous cases, it is convenient to arrange them as follows:

[Statutory declaration]

A company under this Act may be wound up by the court, as herein-after defined, under the following circumstances (that is to say)—

[Cases]

(1) Whenever...

(2) Whenever...

(3) Whenever...

(4) Whenever...

(5) Whenever...

[Statutory declaration]

The expression 'the court', as used in this Part of this Act, shall mean the following authorities (that is to say)—

[Cases]

In the case of a company...

In the case of a company...

In the case of a company...

In all cases of companies...

Provided that...

Sometimes a statement of the cases precedes the statutory declaration—

[Cases]

In the following cases, that is to say—

[Statutory declaration]

(1) Where...

(2) Where...

(3) Where...

A useful example of a case with subordinate clauses stating alternatives and several statutory declarations is found in the Foreign Enlistment Act 1870 as follows—

[Case with subordinate clauses]

If the master or owner of any ship, without the license of her Majesty, knowingly either takes on board, or engages to take on board, or has on board such ship within her Majesty's dominions, any of the following persons, in this Act referred to as illegally enlisted persons ; that is to say—

(1) Any person who...

(2) Any person, being a British subject, who...

(3) Any person who...

[Statutory declaration No 1]

Such master or owner shall be guilty of an offence against this Act, and the following consequences shall ensue; that is to say,

[Statutory declaration No 2]

(1) The offender shall be punishable by fine and imprisonment, or either of such punishments, at the discretion of the court before which the offender is convicted; and imprisonment, if awarded, may be either with or without hard labour; and

[Statutory Declaration No. 3]

(2) Such ship shall be detained until the trial and conviction

or acquittal of the master or owner, and until all penalties inflicted on the master or owner have been paid, or the master or owner has given security for the payment of such penalties to the satisfaction of two justices of the peace, or other magistrate or magistrates having the authority of two justices of the peace; and,

[Statutory declaration No. 4]

(3) All illegally enlisted persons shall immediately on the discovery of the offence be taken on shore, and shall not be allowed to return to the ship.

A case with several alternatives may be expressed as follows:

Merchant Shipping Act 1854, section 45

[Case]

Whenever any change takes place in the registered ownership of any ship, then, if such change occurs at a time when the ship is at her port of registry,

[Statutory Declaration]

the master shall forthwith deliver the certificate of registry to the registrar, and he shall endorse thereon a memorandum of such change;

[Alternative Case]

but if such change occurs during the absence of the ship from her port of registry,

[Statutory Declaration]

then upon her first return to such port the master shall deliver the certificate of registry to the registrar, and he shall endorse thereon a like memorandum of the change;

[Further alternative case]

or if she previously arrives at any port where there is a *British* registrar,

[Statutory declaration (1)]

such registrar shall, upon being advised by the registrar of her port of registry of the change having taken place, endorse a like memorandum thereof on the certificate of registry, and may for that purpose require the certificate to be delivered to him, so that the ship be not thereby detained;

[Statutory Declaration (2)]

and any master who fails to deliver to the registrar the certificate of registry as herein-before required shall incur a penalty not exceeding one hundred pounds.

GENERAL RULE AS TO EXPRESSION OF CASE

The case must always be so expressed as to be clearly distinguishable from the other parts of the sentence. It need not, indeed should not, where the rules of composition require a different arrangement, be comprised in a consecutive sentence.

A separation of the members of a case is almost always desirable where it consists partly of the statement of a fact and partly of an act to be done. This will appear from the following example, in which the case is shown in italics, the statutory declaration in ordinary type:

Irish Church Act 1869, section 25(3)

Where any Church was in use at the time of the passing of this Act, and no application in respect thereof is made by the said representative body of the said church within the said prescribed period, and such church was erected at the private expense of any person, the Commissioners shall, *on the application of the person who erected such church, if alive, or of his representatives if he died since the year one thousand eight hundred,* by order vest such church in the applicant or applicants, or in such person or persons as he or they may direct.

25 Mode of stating conditions

The law frequently confers a benefit or imposes an obligation on certain conditions. A condition is aptly introduced by 'If...' or (where it follows a negative sentence) by 'unless' or 'until'.

> [Case]
>
> Where any person is convicted of an offence
>
> [Condition]
>
> if he has given notice at the prescribed time and in the prescribed manner
>
> [Statutory declaration]
>
> he may appeal from such conviction...

Where the conditions are numerous it is best (as has been before remarked with respect to the case) to state them in separate subordinate sentences.

> *Irish Church Act 1869, section 34*
>
> [Statutory declaration]
>
> The Commissioners may at any time after the first of January one thousand eight hundred and seventy one sell by public auction or private contract, or otherwise convert into money, any real or personal property vested in them by this Act,
>
> [Conditions]
>
> subject to the other provisions of this Act, and to the following conditions—
>
> (1) They shall not sell...
>
> (2) Perpetuity rents shall...
>
> (3) The price of the rights to mines or quarries shall...
>
> (4) They shall not sell to the public...
>
> (5) They shall not sell to the public...

(6) Notice shall be given to...

(7) An owner shall be deemed...

[Case]

Where any person is authorised by any Act of Parliament passed after the commencement of this Act to appeal from the decision of a court of summary jurisdiction to a court of general or quarter sessions,

[Statutory declaration]

he may appeal to such court, subject to the conditions and regulations following—

[Condition 1]

The appeal shall be made...

[Condition 2]

The appeal shall...

[Condition 3]

The appellant shall...

[Condition 4]

Where the appellant...

[Condition 5]

The court of appeal...

[Condition 6]

Whenever a decision...

[Condition 7]

Every notice...

Another mode of stating the conditions in the last-mentioned example would be to substitute for the words 'subject to the conditions and regulations following' the words 'but no appeal shall be entertained *unless* the following conditions and regulations have been complied with'.

The greatest caution must, however, be used in putting a sentence in a negative form, as it makes the performance of the conditions a matter of absolute necessity, and the omission of the smallest portion of them will render the appeal altogether nugatory. On the other hand, if the affirmative expression only be used, the court will consider the enactment as to the conditions directory, and dispense with them on due cause being shown for their omission.

An example of very complicated cases with a condition, attached to the later but not to the earlier statutory declaration, may be found in the Artisans and Labourers Dwellings Improvement Act 1875, section 3.

26 Mode of stating exceptions

The word 'except' may generally be used in introducing exceptions, but care must be taken to avoid its use where it is likely to lead to ambiguity. This is illustrated by section 14 of the Irish Church Bill as brought in—

> The Commissioners shall, as soon as may be after the passing of this Act, ascertain and declare by order the amount of yearly income of which the holder of any archbishopric, bishopric, benefice, or cathedral preferment in or connected with the said Church will be deprived by virtue of this Act, after deducting all rates and taxes, *except income or property tax, salaries of permanent curates employed as herein-after mentioned, payments to diocesan schoolmasters, and other outgoings to which such holder is liable by law.*

In the above example it will be perceived that it was intended only to except income or property tax, but as the sentence is worded it may reasonably be argued that all the substantives that follow the word 'except' are excepted. The sentence should run as follows—

> After deducting all rates and taxes, salaries to permanent curates employed as herein-after mentioned, payments to diocesan schoolmasters, and other outgoings to which such holder is liable by law, but not deducting income or property tax.

Where exceptions are numerous they should (as in the instances of numerous cases and numerous conditions) be placed in separate members of the section or even in a separate section. Where the enumeration of the exception is short, compared with the enumeration of the particulars not excepted, it is often convenient to state the exceptions first.

Illustrations of this may be found in sections 15 and 31 of the Bankruptcy Act 1869:

> The property of the bankrupt divisible amongst his creditors, and in this Act referred to as the property of the bankrupt, shall not comprise the following particulars:
>
> [Exception 1]
>
> (1) Property held by the bankrupt on trust for any other person:
>
> [Exception 2]
>
> (2) The tools (if any) of his trade, and the necessary wearing apparel and bedding of himself, his wife and children, to a value, inclusive of tools and apparel and bedding, not exceeding twenty pounds in the whole:
>
> But it shall comprise the following particulars:
>
> [General enumeration]
>
> (3) All such property as may belong to or be vested in the bankrupt at the commencement of the bankruptcy, or may be acquired by or devolve on him during its continuance:
>
> (4) The capacity to exercise and take proceedings for exercising all such powers in or over or in respect of property as

might have been exercised by the bankrupt for his own benefit at the commencement of his bankruptcy or during its continuance, except the right of nomination to a vacant ecclesiastical benefice:

(5) All goods and chattels being, at the commencement of the bankruptcy, in the possession, order, or disposition of the bankrupt, being a trader, by the consent and permission of the true owner, of which goods and chattels the bankrupt is reputed owner, or of which he has taken upon himself the sale or disposition as owner; provided that things in action, other than debts due to him in the course of his trade or business, shall not be deemed goods and chattels within the meaning of this clause.

Section 31 of Bankruptcy Act 1869

[Further exceptions]

Demands in the nature of unliquidated damages arising otherwise than by reason of a contract or promise shall not be provable in bankruptcy, and no person having notice of any act of bankruptcy available for adjudication against the bankrupt shall prove for any debt or liability contracted by the bankrupt subsequently to the date of his so having notice.

[Further enumeration]

Save as aforesaid, all debts and liabilities, present or future, certain or contingent, to which the bankrupt is subject at the date of the order of adjudication, or to which he may become subject during the continuance of the bankruptcy by reason of any obligation incurred previously to the date of the order of adjudication, shall be deemed to be debts provable in bankruptcy, and may be proved in the prescribed manner before the trustee in the bankruptcy.

On the other hand, in the Debtors Act 1869, section 4, the exceptions, being numerous, are placed at the end of the section:

[Statutory declaration]

No person shall, after the commencement of this Act, be arrested or imprisoned for making default in payment of a sum of money.

There shall be excepted from the operation of the above enactment—

[Exception 1]

(1) Default...

[Exception 2]

(2) Default...

[Exception 3]

(3) Default...

[Exception 4]

(4) Default...

[Exception 5]

(5) Default...

[Exception 6]

(6) Default...

27 Use of provisoes

Provisoes[2] should never be used to define the case or the condition or the legal subject. Their proper function is to make a special exemption from a general statutory declaration, and they should be exclusively confined to that function. The rules with respect to the grouping of conditions and exceptions apply to provisoes also where they are numerous.

---

2   Provisoes are not generally used nowadays.

28 Summary of Rules

To give a short summary of what has been stated. The draftsman should recollect that an enactment, in its most complicated form, is made up of the following parts:

1. The case;
2. The statutory declaration;
3. The conditions;
4. The exceptions;
5. The provisoes.

The arrangement of these parts must much depend on the judgment of the draftsman. The only general rule to be observed is that each part should in substance be clearly distinguishable, and should be comprised, as far as possible, in a short sentence or sentences.[3]

29 Selection of words and other matters

It may be well to give a few miscellaneous suggestions with respect to the selection of words and structure of sentences.

In the selection of words, Latin words and, where possible without a sacrifice of accuracy, technical phraseology should be avoided. The word best adapted to express a thought in ordinary composition will generally be found to be the best that can be used in an Act of Parliament.

---

[3] Where the circumstances under which an enactment is to take effect are complicated, there is no practical difference, except in form, between the statement of the subordinate propositions of the case and conditions. The draftsman must use his discretion in using one or the other form as seems most advisable.

The use of technical phraseology may be admitted in an Act relating to contingent remainders, but should in the case of an Agricultural Holdings Act or Highway Act be excluded from the body of the Act, and if required to be introduced for the purpose of securing legal precision, appear only in the interpretation clause explaining, extending or limiting words in ordinary use, such as 'Agricultural Holding', 'Highway' and so forth.

Law is made for man, and not man for law. It is too often forgotten by lawyers and draftsmen that the majority of Acts of Parliament contain rules of conduct to be observed by illiterate persons and to be enforced by authorities unacquainted with the technical language of Coke and the year books.

A draftsman should pay attention to collecting and arranging for his own use any relative terms, such as 'mortgage, mortgagor, mortgagee'; 'comply, compliance'; 'require, requisition'; and exhaustive forms of expression, such as 'all property, real and personal, including all interests and rights in to or out of property', 'rights, duties, liabilities, capacities and incapacities' and 'acts, neglects, defaults'.

The following miscellaneous remarks may be useful.

Nouns should be used in preference to pronouns, even though the noun has to be repeated. Repetition of the same word is never a fault if an ambiguity is thereby avoided.

An Act of Parliament should be deemed to be always speaking, and therefore the present or past tense should be adopted. And 'shall' should be used as an *imperative* only — and not as a *future*.

'If' should be followed by the indicative where it suggests a case. For example, 'If any person commits... he shall be punished as follows.'

Where there is an enumeration of several persons or things, followed by an enactment intended to apply to all and each of them, care must be taken to make this enactment apply both generally and distributively. For instance, 'A, B, C and D, or any of them may...' or 'any one or more of the following persons may &...'.

It must be recollected that 'other' following an enumeration of various particulars is always construed to mean other things of the like description as those before enumerated, unless the construction be negatived by the introduction of words such as 'whether of the same kind as, &c, or not'.

Numbers should be written at full length. Thus sections of an Act should be cited as 'section two' etc.[4]

The titles, as well as the year and chapter of Acts should, for the sake of accuracy, be given. Where an Act is cited by its short title a reference should always be made in the margin to its session and chapter.[5]

Lastly, the same thing should invariably be said in the same words.

30 Recommendation of use of generic terms

It will often be found that it is absolutely essential to shorten a sentence by giving a generic name to several particulars.

---

4 This is no longer the case. The form 'section 2' is now used.

5 Chapter numbers of Acts and, in Scotland, asp numbers of Acts of the Scottish Parliament are no longer included.

Take, for example, the Inclosure Act 1876. It was desirable that the Commissioners should not make a provisional order for the inclosure of a common until they had satisfied themselves that the inclosure would be for the benefit not only of the public in general but of the inhabitants of the neighbourhood.

In order to simplify the language of the Act, the generic terms 'benefit of the neighbourhood and private interests' were used to cover the following subjects:

> the health, comfort and convenience of the inhabitants of any cities, towns and villages or populous places in or near any parish in which the land proposed to be inclosed, or any part thereof, may be situate (hereinafter included under the expression 'the benefit of the neighbourhood'), as to the advantage of the persons interested in the common to which such application relates (hereinafter included under the expression 'private interests').

Again, in Bills respecting various local areas a system was adopted of grouping the areas and the spending authorities under the term local areas and local authorities, setting forth in a schedule the separate names of the areas and authorities.

Not infrequently a difficulty may be avoided by nicknaming, as it were, a particular person or body of persons, so as to comprise in one word what would otherwise make a complicated sentence.

Take for an example section 66 of the Prison Act 1865:

> Where a prison authority, in this section called *the contracting authority*, has contracted with any other prison authority, in this section called *the receiving authority*, that *the receiving authority* is to receive into and maintain in its prison any prisoners maintainable at the expense of *the contracting authority*, the prison

of *the receiving authority* shall for all the purposes of and incidental to the commitment, trial, detention, and punishment of the prisoners of *the contracting authority*, or any of such purposes, according to the tenor of the contract, be deemed to be the prison of *the contracting authority*, except that *the contracting authority* shall have no right to interfere in the management of the prison of *the receiving authority*.

A little consideration will show that if the words 'contracting authority' and 'receiving authority' were not adopted, the sentence would be overloaded with words to such an extent as to be unintelligible. In short, whenever a draftsman finds his sentence becoming confused, although he has duly observed the directions as to the statement of the case, the conditions, and so forth, he may be certain that some part of it wants to be separated from the rest, and to be dealt with as a separate paragraph at the end of the section, or even as a separate section.

The framer of the Volunteer Act 1869 obviously saw the difficulty of stating in section 3 the mode in which the demand was to be made as it comprised so many particulars that it would, if introduced into the beginning of that section, have inconveniently separated the several members of the case. Accordingly he lightened section 3 by inserting in that section the words 'on demand made as herein-after mentioned' and placed the particulars of the demand in section 4.

A similar course was adopted in the Artisans and Labourers Dwellings Improvement Act 1875. On referring to the Act it will be found that the action of the local authority under section 3 is to take place 'when an official representation as herein-after mentioned' is made as to the unhealthiness of the area and so forth.

The nature of the official representation referred to in section 3 is stated in section 4.

A reference to the Act will show that if section 4 had formed part of section 3 the case would have been so overcrowded with words as to be absolutely unintelligible.

A form of section that deserves to be considered by a draftsman, as an example of the advantage to be derived from getting a generic term to express and include a number of special predicates, is section 346 of the Merchant Shipping Act 1854:

> Every pilot boat or ship shall be distinguished by the following *characteristics*; (that is to say,)
>
> (1) A black colour painted or tarred outside...
>
> (2) On her stern the name of the owner thereof and the port to which she belongs painted in white letters, and on each bow the number of the licence of such boat or ship:
>
> (3) When afloat, a flag at the masthead or on a sprit, or staff...
>
> And it shall be the duty of the master of such boat or ship to attend to the following *particulars*: First, that the boat or ship possesses all the above *characteristics;* secondly, that the aforesaid flag is kept clean and distinct, so as to be easily discerned at a proper distance; and lastly, that the names and numbers before mentioned are not at any time concealed; and if default is made in any of the above particulars he shall incur a penalty not exceeding twenty pounds for each default.

The generic term *characteristics* prevents the necessity for a repetition of the subsections (1), (2) and (3). Similarly the declaration that 'it shall be the duty of the master to attend to the following particulars' and the infliction of the penalty on default being made 'in any of the above particulars' makes the master liable, first, for a general default in the boat not possessing the characteristics required; and, secondly, for a special default in not attending to the flag being kept clean, and so forth.

Section 48 of the same Act illustrates the advantage of the use of the word 'event' where a set of circumstances have to be repeated:

> *In the event* of the certificate of registry of any ship being mislaid, lost, or destroyed, if such *event* occurs at any port of the United Kingdom, &c, then the registrar of her port of registry shall grant a new certificate of registry in lieu of and as a substitute for her original certificate of registry; but if such *event* occurs elsewhere, the master or some other person having knowledge of the circumstances shall make a declaration, &c.; and the registrar shall thereupon grant a provisional certificate, &c.

If the word 'event' were not used, it would require a constant repetition of the words 'certificate of registry of any ship being mislaid, lost, or destroyed'.

31 Enumeration of particulars

In framing an Act intended to include a great number of particulars, no attempt should be made to enumerate the particulars, but a generic term should be used dealing exhaustively with the subject-matter of the Act.

Those particulars only should be enumerated which are intended to be excepted from the Act.

For example, the Succession Duty Act is framed with a view to including every disposition or devolution of property at death that is not subject to the Legacy Duty Acts. It was impossible to make any exhaustive enumeration of the particulars of the property to be included in the Act. The course, therefore, was adopted of including in the Act every possible disposition or devolution of property on death, and then to exempt from the operation of the Act any acquisition of property in respect of which duty was payable under the Legacy Duty Acts.

The most frequent cause of ambiguity in Acts of Parliament is the lack of an adjectival inflexion.

For example, the expression 'Every factory and every workshop subject to this Act' raises the question whether 'subject to this Act' applies to both or to the last only of the nouns. If it is intended to apply to the last only, the ambiguity is avoided by placing the qualified noun before the unqualified, that is to say, by reading the sentence 'Every workshop subject to this Act and every factory'. To make the qualification certainly apply to both, the form of sentence must be altered somewhat in this way:

> Where a factory and a workshop are subject to this Act they shall...

The same difficulty arises in the case of the relative, e.g., 'In a factory or workshop in which young children are employed' is an expression subject to the same ambiguity, which can only be avoided by adopting a similar rule to that recommended above, or else by repeating the antecedent, and reading the sentence:

> Every factory and workshop in which factory and workshop young children are employed.

Illustrations might be multiplied indefinitely. The draftsman cannot do better than read carefully Mr Coode's book on legislative expression referred to above. He might also study, for forms of expression, the Code of Criminal

Procedure and Civil Procedure of the State of New York, and the General Rules of the Court of Chancery of 8 May 1845.

He should analyse the arrangement of Acts, and pick to pieces sentences which appear to him to be well drawn. As a model of clarity of expression, no better example can be found than Paley's work on Moral Philosophy.[6] A book which will well repay a careful perusal by a draftsman, indeed by every writer of business compositions, is *Errors in the Use of English* by WB Hodgson.[7]

---

[6] Paley, William (1743–1805). *The Principles of Moral and Political Philosophy* (1785).

[7] Hodgson, William Ballantyne (1815–1880). *Errors in the Use of English*, ed. Emily Hodgson (Edinburgh: David Douglas, 1882).

CHAPTER FOUR

GENERAL OBSERVATIONS

The object of this chapter is to explain certain formal parts and groups of sections constantly recurring in Acts of Parliament.

32 Preamble

The proper function of a preamble[1] is to explain certain facts which are necessary to be explained before the enactments contained in the Act can be understood.

For example, the Courts of Justice Building Act 1865 proposes to apply certain funds to the payment of the expenses of constructing new courts of justice. Accordingly, a long preamble is prefixed to the Act, explaining the origin of those funds, for without such a preamble it would have been impossible for Parliament to have understood the subject-matter of the Act.

Preambles are also not infrequently required in amending Acts for the purpose of showing the exact bearing of the amendments on the principal Act.

A preamble may also be used to limit the scope of certain expressions in an Act.

For example, in dealing with the subject of licensing public-houses, it may be convenient in the preamble to

---

[1] Acts do not generally have preambles nowadays.

define as licensing Acts the Acts relating to the sale of intoxicating liquors.

Sometimes a preamble is inserted for political reasons when the object of an Act is popular and admits of being stated in a telling sentence or sentences.

Other cases will occur in practice in which a preamble will be found convenient to explain a fact or introduce a definition; but it is not as a general rule advisable to enunciate the principle of an Act in a preamble, as the opponents of the Act are sure to select it as a battle-ground instead of dividing on the actual provisions of the Act.

33 Short title of Act

Every Act should have a short title, ending with the date of the year in which it is passed.

34 Extent of Act

Where an Act is intended to operate within the territorial limits of the United Kingdom but not beyond, there is no necessity for a section declaring the extent of the Act.[2] The most frequent use of such a section is to restrict the Act to England by declaring that it shall not extend to Scotland or Ireland. Sometimes, however, an affirmative extension is required, declaring that it is to extend to the Channel Islands, the Colonies, her Majesty's dominions in India, and so forth.

---

[2] The position on extent sections has altered over the years, most recently as a result of the devolution settlements of 1999, when Acts providing for the devolution of legislative powers to Scotland, Northern Ireland and Wales came into force.

Wales and Berwick-upon-Tweed are included in England by the Act of 20 Geo. II c.42 and ought not therefore to be specially mentioned.

The phrase that an Act shall apply to 'England only' is not advisable, as it would seem to exclude by inference the inclusion in England of Wales and Berwick-upon-Tweed established by the above mentioned Act of 20 Geo. II.

35 Commencement of Act

At common law every Act of Parliament commences from the first day of the session in which it is passed. The injustice arising from such a rule was obviated by 33 Geo. III. c.13. It enacts that the Clerk of the Parliaments shall endorse after the title of the Act the date, month and year when the same is passed and receives the Royal Assent, and that such endorsement shall be taken to be part of such Act, and to be the date of its commencement where no other commencement is therein provided.

Even thus, great inconvenience arises from bringing a complicated Act into operation immediately on the date of its passing, and it is almost always advisable to postpone its operation for some little time, in order at all events that the public may become acquainted with its provisions.

The 1st of January following the passing of the Act is the most natural day for bringing it into operation, when there are no special reasons to be adduced in favour of another day. If, however, the Act commences at a future period there should usually be inserted a provision giving immediate effect to any rules, appointments of officers or other machinery required to bring the Act duly into operation at the date of its commencement.

36 Interpretation of terms

The interpretation clause should be preceded by a qualifying introductory clause, such as 'In this Act, unless the context otherwise requires'.

In framing definitions and other subsidiary clauses regard should be had to the Interpretation Act 1889 which is set out in the appendix,[3] and which must be learnt by heart by the draftsman. Definitions require to be carefully considered, as a misuse of them is a frequent cause of ambiguity. It should be recollected that a word once defined preserves its meaning throughout the whole Act — a truism frequently overlooked in practice.

A word should never be defined to mean something which it does not properly include, e.g., 'piracy' ought not to be defined to include 'mutiny' and so forth.

The fewer the definitions the better. As a general rule, the draftsman should endeavour to draw his Act without definitions, and insert them only when he finds that they are absolutely necessary.

The proper use of definitions is to include or exclude something with respect to the inclusion or exclusion of which there is a doubt without such a definition. No attempt should be made to make a pretence of scientific precision by defining words of which the ordinary meaning is sufficiently clear and exact for the purpose of the Act in which they are used.

---

3 The Interpretation Act 1889 is not reproduced in this edition.

37 As to place in Act of definitions and certain other preliminary matters

The above-mentioned sections must be placed either at the beginning or the end of the Act. Logically, their proper place is the beginning of the Act, as the reader cannot understand the Act till he is master of the definitions or explanations of the terms used in the Act. Politically, their proper place is at the end of the Act, as a definition frequently narrows or widens the whole scope of an Act. Parliament cannot possibly judge whether such narrowing or widening is or is not expedient till they are acquainted with the Act itself.

For example, in the Contagious Diseases (Animals) Act 1869, the definition, as it is called, of local authorities in Schedule 2 determines the persons by whom, the places in which, and the funds out of which the whole Act is to be carried into operation.

This logical and political antagonism of arrangement might easily be reconciled were it the custom of Parliament to postpone the above sections in the same way as they postpone the preamble till the Bill has been gone through. Such a postponement, however, would, in a hardly fought Bill, give rise to a division. The draftsman, therefore, is recommended as a general rule to adhere to the political and not to the logical rule and to place the sections in question at the end of the Act.

38 Adjustment of existing and new law

One of the most responsible duties of a draftsman is to provide for the adjustment of the provisions of the new Act which he is drawing, and the former law.

Take a very simple case, the New Forest Act 1877. The instructions to the draftsman would be to amend the constitution of the Court of Verderers[4] by increasing the number of verderers to seven, one of whom should be nominated by the Crown, and the others be elected, the elective verderers to be chosen by the parliamentary electors of the parishes and townships within the confines of the Forest, and by the commoners.

The principles of this instruction are carried into effect by sections 14–23, defining the constitution of the verderers, the qualification of the electors, the time at which the verderers come into office and their legal status. The details of their election are contained in Schedules 2 and 3, providing for a register of commoners and the mode of election of the verderers.

An examination of these clauses will show the necessity for the draftsman filling in the details of an instruction by sections which, though in one sense formal, in another require to be settled with great consideration. The draftsman must carefully look forward and see that the new body will be brought into action at the time fixed for the determination of the old body, and that there is no hiatus between the old and the new administration.

Frequently, however, more complicated cases arise in which provisions have to be inserted for abolishing an old authority and constituting a new one.

Take, for example, the Supreme Court of Judicature Act 1873, in which the greater portion of the Act is occupied in

---

[4] The Verderers (Lat. *viridis*, green) are judicial officers of the New Forest who sit monthly as a court to protect and conserve its flora and fauna.

the transfer of jurisdiction of the existing courts and the existing officers, and the declaration of the status of the existing officers when so transferred.

39 Exemptions and savings

Where a new law is laid down establishing penalties on new manufactures, or bringing established manufactures within the jurisdiction of an administrative body, a separate heading of exemptions and savings will usually be required.

An illustration of this necessity will be found in sections 97–103 of the Explosives Act 1875. These sections provide, among other things, for the exemption of Government factories, for cases of emergency in which a master of a ship or carrier transgresses the law by stress of weather or inevitable accident. They further reserve, in sections 102–103, the common law liabilities in respect of nuisances and the powers of local Acts.

Provisions such as these must always be kept in mind by the draftsman, and should be inserted by him when necessary without special instructions.

The section which most frequently raises the question of savings is that of the repeal of Acts. As a general rule, when Acts are repealed, existing appointments and existing rights or privileges are maintained, and offences committed under the old Acts are punished in pursuance of the old provisions.

Frequently, however, the draftsman will have to deviate from the above-mentioned rule. He will be required to abolish the old officers instead of retaining them, or to declare that the procedure of the new Acts is to be substituted in relation to the punishment of offences committed before the Act for the procedure under the old Acts and so forth.

In short, he must be prepared to reconcile the provisions of the old and the new law by the insertion of such provisions as his legal knowledge will show him to be necessary for the proper working of the law.

The difficulty of settling the repeal clause of an Act is enhanced rather than diminished by the enactment of section 38 of the Interpretation Act 1889.

That section, which is copied from the statutory forms framed for the use of the Parliamentary Counsel Office, makes provision for the usual incidents attending a repeal, but at the same time if the proposed Act is intended to affect existing rights or interests which are excluded by the Interpretation Act, care must be taken to say that such portion of the Interpretation Act as contains such exclusions shall not apply.

It may be well to suggest here a provision which is often forgotten, viz., that in drawing a temporary Act which is to expire on a given day, and which imposes penalties or creates obligations, care must be taken to provide that offences committed and obligations incurred before the day appointed for its expiration may be punished or enforced after that day, or else the law will, in a great degree, fail in its purpose.

40 Schedules

Great care should be taken in the preparation of schedules.

It is desirable to include in a schedule matters of detail. It is improper to put in a schedule matters of principle.

The drawing of the proper line of demarcation between the two classes of matters is often difficult. All that can be said is that nothing should be placed in a schedule to which the attention of Parliament should be particularly directed.

For example, the *constitution* of an electoral or financial body of persons should be found in the body of the Act. But the mode of conducting the election of the electoral body, and the rules as to proceedings at meetings of the financial body, may not improperly be placed in a schedule.

41 Alterations during passage of Act

Great care must be taken in noticing any consequential alterations that may be required in consequence of amendments made in the passage of an Act through Parliament.

For example, if a schedule is taken out, nothing is more common than to find that the omission is noticed in one section, but the number of the schedules is forgotten to be altered in another section. Hence, the schedules are misnumbered, and most important sections may fail in effect.

With a view to obviate this difficulty, the draftsman should note in the margin of each schedule the sections in which it is mentioned, and should refer to that note in the event of an alteration being made in any of such sections.

Similarly with respect to dates, the alteration of a date in one section not infrequently necessitates the alteration of a date in another. This is forgotten in the haste of passing the Act through committee, and unless the alteration is attended to by the draftsman, the Act fails in effect in some material provision.

INDEX

Act of Parliament, definition of
   term as used in work, 42
   deemed to be always speaking, 91
Acts, simple and complex,
   definition of, 43
Adjustment of existing and new
   law, 103
Administration of the law, rule as
   to position in Act of provisions
   relating to, 53
Alterations, during passage of Act,
   107
American works on legal
   expression, 19
Arrangement of subject-matter of
   Act, Chap. Two, 45
   selection and statement of
      principles, 45, 52
   illustrations, 47–52
   general rules of, 53–9
   summary of rules, 59
   observations on reference from
      one part of an Act to
      another, 62
   division of Act into parts, and
      grouping under headings, 70
   extent of, 100
   commencement of, 101
   construction of, 102
   place of various provisions, 103
Austin, Mr, views on technical and
   ethical legislation, 15, 18

Cairns, Lord, appoints Statute Law
   Committee, 28

Cardwell, Mr, Merchant Shipping
   Bill, 20
Case, mode of stating the, 79
   and statutory declarations, 80
   with subordinate clauses, 81
   with several alternative cases, 82
   general rule as to expression of, 83
   with conditions, 84
Case law, distinction between
   leading cases and illustrative
   cases, 40
Clarity, the object of parliamentary
   drafting, 73
Code, remarks as to framing, 35
Codification, 28
   meaning of term and remarks as
      to, 32–3
Colonial Bill for Sir W.
   Molesworth, 20
Commencement of Act, 101
Common law, advice as to studying
   the, 41
Composition of sentences, Chap.
   Three, 73
Complex Acts, definition of, 43
Conditions, mode of stating, 84
   mode of stating, where
      numerous, 84
Consolidation of law, 28–9
Consolidation Acts, incorporation
   of, 66
   grouping sections in, 70
Construction of Act, 102
Coode's Legislative Expression, 73
   n.1

Darlington Improvement Act, cited, 18
Dates, care to be taken as to alteration of, 107
Defining clause, use of, with generic term, 63–4
Definitions, use of, 102
　place of in Act, 103
Disraeli, Mr, his methods, 23–4
Division of Acts into Parts and headings, 70
Draftsman, mode in which he should prepare himself to draw Act, 38
　further advice to, 97–8

Enactments, definition of, 43
　observations as to mode of framing principal and sub-ordinate, 51, 56
　simplest forms of, 73
　mode of grouping independent, of a simple character, 76
　mode of grouping a number of short, in one section, 77
　summary of rules as to composition of, 59
English Acts, mode of applying to Scotland and Ireland, 63
English law, remarks as to substance and form of, 38
Enumeration of several persons or things enactment applying to, 75
Enumeration of particulars, 96
'Except', use of the word, 86
Exceptions, mode of stating, 86
　where numerous, 87
Exemptions and savings, 105
Exhaustive forms of expression, advice as to collecting and arranging, 91
Existing and new law, adjustment of, 103
Extent of Act, 100

Formal Parts of Acts, Chap. Four, 99
Frauds, Statute of, cited, 18
General Observations, Chap. Four, 99
Generic terms, use of, 92
　expressing and including a number of special predicates, 95
Gladstone, Mr, views on drafting, 21–3
　quoted, 27
Grouping, legal subjects, and predicates, 75
　independent enactments of a simple character, 76
　a number of short enactments in one section, 77
　clauses under headings, 70

Headings, division of Acts under, 70
'Herein-after', 'Herein-before' objections to use of, 69
Hodgson's 'Errors in the Use of English', 98

Illustrations of selection and statement of principles in simple and complex Acts, 49–52
Incorporation of Consolidation Acts, 66
Independent enactments, mode of grouping, 76

Interpretation Act, 1889, the, 106
Introductory observations, Chap. One, 38

Lands Clauses Acts, incorporation of, 66
Langton, Stephen, as draftsman, 17
Law, method of getting up, 39
Legal subject and predicate, definition of, 73
Local and exceptional provisions, rule as to position of, in Act, 57

Marginal notes, observations on, 72
Mathew, Lord Justice, extract from judgment in *Kaill* v *Towse*, 68
'May', use of the word, 74
Method of getting up statute law, 39
   case law, 40
Molesworth, Sir Wm, Colonial Bill, 20

New York code, 97–8
Nouns, to be used instead of pronouns, 91
Numbers, to be written at full length, 92

'Other', construction of, 92

Paley's 'Moral Philosophy', 98
Particulars, enumeration of, 96
Parts and headings, division of Acts into, 70
Preamble, object of, 99
Predicates, definition of, and mode of grouping legal, 73, 75

Principal enactments, mode of framing, 51
Principles, on which Act is based, selection and statement of, 45
   illustrations in case of simple Acts, 47
   in case of complex Acts, 49
Procedure, rule as to position in Act of provisions as to, 58
Proposition, rule as to position in Act of simple and complex, less and greater, 55
Provisions declaring the law, rule as to position of, in Act, 53
   relating to administration of the law, rule as to position of, in Act, 53
   local and exceptional, rule as to, 57
   temporary, rule as to, 57
   relating to repeal of Acts, rule as to, 57
   referential, 62, 66, 68
Provisoes, use of, 89

Reddendo singula singulis, necessity for adoption of rule to be avoided, 65
Referential provisions, observations on, where reference made to another part of same Act, 62
   observations on, where reference made to other Acts, 66
   Lord Justice Mathew on, 68
Referential words, expressions to be avoided, 69
Reform Bill, the, of 1867, history of its preparation, 23 *et seq.*

Relative terms, advice as to collecting and arranging, 91
Repeal of Acts, and savings, 105
Repetition, better than ambiguity, 91
Rules of arrangement of an Act,
  Rule 1, 53
  Rule 2, 55
  Rule 3, 56
  Rule 4, 57
  Rule 5, 58
  summary of, 59
  as to mode of stating the case, 79
  as to selection of words and other matters, 90

Savings, sections containing, 105
  in repeal clause, 105–6
Schedules, proper use of, 106
Selection and statement of principles on which Acts are based 45, 52
Selection of words and other matters, 90
Sentences, composition of, Chap. 3, 73
'Shall', use of the word, 74
Short title, expediency of, 100
Simple Acts, definition of, 43
Statement of case, 79
  of conditions, 84
  of exceptions, 86
Statutory declarations, with various forms of cases, 80
Stephen, Mr Justice, on drafting, 27
Subject-matter of Act, arrangement of, Chap. 2, 45
Subject and predicate, definition of, 73

grouping legal subjects and predicates, 75
Subordinate enactments, mode of framing, 51
Subordinate subject, rule where provisions of principal subject are wholly or partially applicable to, 62
Summary of general rules of arrangement of an Act, and observations, 53–9
  of rules as to enactments, 90

Technical Phraseology, how far admissible, 90
Temporary Act, provision as to offences committed and obligations incurred before expiration of, 106
Temporary provisions, rule as to position of, in Act, 57
Terms used in work, explanation of certain, 42
Titles of Acts, citation of, 92
  short, 100

Wales, included in England by statute, 101
Westcott, Dr (Bishop of Durham), on verbal criticism, 16
Words, selection of, 90

Luath Press Limited
committed to publishing well written books worth reading

LUATH PRESS takes its name from Robert Burns, whose little collie Luath (*Gael.*, swift or nimble) tripped up Jean Armour at a wedding and gave him the chance to speak to the woman who was to be his wife and the abiding love of his life. Burns called one of 'The Twa Dogs' Luath after Cuchullin's hunting dog in Ossian's *Fingal*. Luath Press was established in 1981 in the heart of Burns country, and now resides a few steps up the road from Burns' first lodgings on Edinburgh's Royal Mile.

Luath offers you distinctive writing with a hint of unexpected pleasures.

Most bookshops in the UK, the US, Canada, Australia, New Zealand and parts of Europe either carry our books in stock or can order them for you. To order direct from us, please send a £sterling cheque, postal order, international money order or your credit card details (number, address of cardholder and expiry date) to us at the address below. Please add post and packing as follows: UK – £1.00 per delivery address; overseas surface mail – £2.50 per delivery address; overseas airmail – £3.50 for the first book to each delivery address, plus £1.00 for each additional book by airmail to the same address. If your order is a gift, we will happily enclose your card or message at no extra charge.

Luath Press Limited
543/2 Castlehill
The Royal Mile
Edinburgh EH1 2ND
Scotland

Telephone: 0131 225 4326 (24 hours)
email: sales@luath.co.uk
Website: www.luath.co.uk